The Mystery Fancier

Volume 6, Number 1
January/February, 1983

TABLE OF CONTENTS

MYSTERIOUSLY SPEAKING 1
Captain Joseph T. Shaw's *Black Mask* Scrapbook,
   by E.R. Hagemann. 2
Detection by Other Means, by Bob Sampson. 7
Joe Orton's and Tom Stoppard's Burlesques of the
   Detective Genre, by Earl F. Bargainnier 18
Bloody Balaclava: Charlotte MacLeod's Campus Comedy
   Mysteries, by Jane S. Bakerman. 23
Spy Series Characters in Hardback, Part XIII,
   by Barry Van Tilburg. 30
IT'S ABOUT CRIME, by Marvin Lachman 32
REEL MURDERS: Movie Reviews by Walter Albert. 36
VERDICTS: Book Reviews. 39
THE DOCUMENTS IN THE CASE: Letters. 43

The Mystery Fancier
(USPS:428-590)
is edited and published bi-monthly by
Guy M. Townsend
1711 Clifty Drive
Madison, IN 47250

SUBSCRIPTION RATES: Domestic second-class mail, $12.00 per year (six issues); first-class mail, U.S. and Canada, $15.00; overseas surface mail, $12.00; overseas airmail, $18.00. Overseas subscribers please pay in international money order, check drawn on U.S. bank, or currency; no checks drawn of foreign banks, please.

Single copy price: $2.50

Second class postage paid at Madison, Indiana

Copyright 1983 by Guy M. Townsend
All rights reserved for contributors
ISSN:0146-3160

Paulette Greene's publication of Madeleine B. Stern's phrenological study of Sherlock Holmes and Sir Arthur Conan Doyle, *The Game's a Head*, mentioned several issues earlier in these pages, has now come to pass. Beautifully printed on fine paper in wraps with illustrations by Sam Greene, this slim (x + 24 pp.) volume is a must for Sherlockians. The price for one of the 500 numbered copies is $15.00, plus $1.50 for postage and insurance. Checks to Paulette Greene Rare Books, 140 Princeton Road, Rockville Centre, NY 11570.
I've a few more new publications to call to your attention. Fans of Arthur W. Upfield's Napoleon Bonaparte novels will rejoice to learn that Philip T. Asdell (5719 Jefferson Blvd., Frederick, MD 21701) is now publishing *The Bony Bulletin*. At $3 for three issues, it's a real bargain.
And Donald Westlake fans will be similarly delighted to learn of the birth of *the ParkerPhile*, a journal devoted to the appreciation of Westlake's many and varied talents. It is edited and published by D. Kingsley Hahn, 1495 Magnolia Ave. E. #2, St. Paul, MN 55106. Bimonthly, it costs $5 a year.
Jiro Kimura advises that *The Maltese Falcon Flyer*, the monthly newsletter of "The Maltese Falcon Society (Japan)," is available to overseas subscribers for $25 surface or $40 air. One problem, though: it's all in Japanese. See this issue's letter column for Jiro's address.
I've been intending to mention Charles Kiddle's *Guide to the First Editions of Edgar Wallace* for some time but haven't had room. Published in a limited edition of 1,000 numbered copies by The Ivory Head Press, Motcombe, Dorset, UK, at ₤3.95, this 88-page, perfect-bound (in wraps), profusely illustrated (with dj illos) book is available in the U.S. from Karen La Porte's Silver Door, 901 Hermosa Ave., Hermosa Beach, CA 90254. I don't know the price in U.S. dollars. An essential work for the Wallace collector.
Bo۰.'ing Green University's Popular Press (Bowling Green, OH 434ι 3) continues its splendid work. Just received are *Murder She Wrote: A Study of Agatha Christie's Detective Fiction*, by Patricia D. Maida and Nicholas B. Spornick ($7.95 paper, $15.95 cloth), and *The Dime Novel Detective*, edited by Gary Hoppenstand ($9.95 paper, $18.95 cloth). Write to the Popular Press for a complete catalogue.
And Scribner's has just issued Ev Bleiler's *Treasury of Victorian Detective Stories* in paper for $9.95.

Captain Joseph T. Shaw's Black Mask Scrapbook
By E.R. Hagemann

Of any given twenty crime novels published in the last year, the best could easily be surpassed by any of the following--none of whom you have probably ever heard of--James Moynahan, Roger Torrey, Francis Cockrell 3d, W.T. Ballard, George H. Coxe and myself, in my humble opinion.... Because we are pulp writers do not despise us too quickly.... In comparison to the crime stories that are being published today as books *and* in smooth-paper magazines--a selection of the stories printed in the pulps will stand up in a manner that will surprise you.
--Letter from John Lawrence, printed in John Chamberlain's column, "Books of the Times," 2 April 1934, *The New York Times*.

What John Lawrence says here is what Cap Shaw (1874-1952) had been saying for some years. While he was editor of *Black Mask*, from 1926 to 1936, he desultorily kept a scrapbook, abetted by a clipping service, which covered roughly the years 1929-1936, or what can be called its golden age. Numbering approximately sixty-three pages and measuring about fourteen by eleven inches, it is a hodgepodge of dated and undated newspaper clips, little-known book reviews, movie reviews, interviews, stills, photos, magazine articles, ads for books published by his stars, letters, blurbs or plants for *Black Mask* in various newspapers--anything and everything that pertained to his beloved rough-paper magazine *and* himself, including stories about his love for fishing and hiking in the Appalachians. In no way would Shaw have disputed Lawrence (who was a contributor to *Black Mask*); in fact, by way of the scrapbook and the public press, Shaw was seeking redress of what he construed to be wrongs and abuses by the Mystery-Detective-Crime Fiction Establishment and American fiction in general.

In no particular order or sequence, the Scrapbook can be conveniently divided into four subject areas: Dashiell Hammett, Raoul F. Whitfield, *Black Mask*, and Shaw. (The latter two will be examined in this article.) There are even a few bonuses, such as data on such *Black Mask* stand-bys as Frederick L. Nebel and Earl and Marion Scott and the discovery of pulp, smooth-paper, and hardback fictioneer Eugene Cunningham as an articulate and literate book reviewer in, of all unlikely places, El Paso, Texas, where he conducted a regular Sunday column. He just happened to be a *Black Mask* regular.

The result of all this is a lode, granted not a mother lode but nearly so, of information that ought to be mined by pulp-fiction devotees.[1] Captain Shaw (a title from World War I) was a promoter, pure and simple, of his magazine. He had to be, for competition was fierce from all sides, particularly in the late twenties and early thirties. One technique he used, and one which was effective, was the "plant" or "blurb" in sundry newspapers out in the hinterlands far removed from his Madison Avenue office. Here is a typical plant which he no doubt wrote himself:

> Black Mask ... is a magazine of thrills. It contains western, detective and adventure stories written by some of the leading writers.... It is a guaranteed thrill feature and gives full value. Short stories and continued novels. Mystery stories predominate but adventure yarns are not far behind. Black Mask holds a promise each month of more good things to come.... The magazine is just the sort of thing needed to relax into from the worries of a hard day.

This was in the 29 May 1930 issue of the Sioux Falls, South Dakota, *Daily Argus-Leader*. Shaw wrote similar items for papers in St. Petersburg, Detroit, Denver, Boston, Newark, Asheville, New York City, Omaha, etc. He would send along a copy of the latest *Mask* as a come-on to say more. It is not clear whether Shaw dispatched the material or whether he employed an advertising agency. Chances are he did it himself. Money was tight and staffs were very small. These blurbs were important for like any pulp *Mask* depended almost solely on newsstand sales; subscriptions were few. The going price was 20¢ per issue, but it dropped to 15¢ as the Great Depression deepened.

By 1930, Shaw had a stable of writers who contributed regularly (Gardner, Hammett, Nebel, Whitfield, et al.), but he was always on the prowl for new talent, and another technique he employed to bring attention to *Mask* was the insert-ad in professional journals, such as *Writer's Digest*. Promoter that he was, Shaw knew exactly what he wanted or needed.

> *Black Mask*, 587 Madison Ave., New York City. Editor, Joseph T. Shaw. Uses shorts of 4000 to 8000 words, and novelettes 10,000 to 15,000 words. One of the very finest markets for the gangster story there is, and Mr. Shaw will give you a square deal and a very prompt decision always. He pays around 1¢ a word, on acceptance. But don't try to wish any mediocre stuff on this editor --you've got to be good! Simple, clipped style preferred to fine writing, so don't use any fancy language. Your detectives and gangsters, above all, must sound *authentic*; their dialogue must *ring the gong*. Study the magazine--*hard*--before you aim at it! --*Writer's Digest*, September 1930; italics in original.

In the next issue, Shaw made a few corrections and said that "two cents a word up would come nearer the fact," adding that rates varied "with the manner in which the particular story" expressed his purpose as editor. Which alluded, I think, to his stable and not to "outsiders."

Not only was he a fierce competitor for sales, he was also a fierce defender of his product. Anything, so long as it was in the limelight, however briefly. Apparently some local comstockery group had complained that the pulps presented crime in a glamorous manner. Shaw took immediate umbrage in a letter to the editor in the September 1930 *Writer's Digest* and insisted that *Mask* had published only one story "in which the gangster was in any sense the 'hero'" and that was Hammett's *Glass Key* and even there virtue came out on top. "*Black Mask* never has and never will make money or attempt to make money by appealing to the appetite for stories which present crime and criminals ... in alluring light; our policy is and always will be the exact opposite."

Let us skip forward a few years for another look at this combative editor. In June 1933 there appeared in the sophisticated *Vanity Fair* an illustrated article on the pulps which was very condescending in tone.[2] Now, *Mask* was not mentioned (but one cover was reproduced). Inference was enough, and Shaw rose to the bait in a *Mask* editorial like a salmon after a Palmer dry fly:

> We venture to assert that *Vanity Fair* itself would not find too favorable comparison between its regular ... writers and those of *Black Mask*.... Again ... we very much doubt if *Vanity Fair* pays on the average its ... writers as much as *Black Mask* pays regularly for *its* stories.... We become a little weary when a careless member of the so-called class magazine fraternity parades its snootiness at the risk of rank misconception.

Next month, Cunningham, at his desk down in El Paso, chimed in by saying that his idea of hell would be a maroon on a desert isle whose only reading was *Vanity Fair*! Editor Frank Crowninshield never accepted Shaw's challenge to publish his rates for fiction and articles.

On the other hand, let someone in the "fraternity" hand out a compliment for *Mask* and old Captain Joe was right there to react. In May 1931 Curtis Patterson, book reviewer for *Town & Country*, was full of praise, saying that Hammett and Whitfield were "as important in the history of picaresque fictions of which the murder-mystery is obviously a part" as were Cézanne and Matisse in art. Said Patterson: "I know very well these are wild and whirling words." Shaw proudly used them in another editorial comment in *Mask*, as he did also with some of Burton Rascoe's remarks in another "class magazine," *Arts & Decoration* (1931):

> Hammett ... worked out his scheme of things in *Black Mask*, and, because he has a narrative gift,... he has emerged as the most talked about of contemporary writers of detective fiction.... Another writer Mr. Shaw has nurtured and developed ... is Raoul Whitfield,... so far ... a notch below Hammett as a character creator and ... not as careful a writer,... but he is inventive and dramatic and his hard-boiled people are hard-boiled people.

Shaw's "aide-de-camp," Gene Cunningham, could always be counted on to help the cause. In his column for 13 September 1931, he has the skipper saying that he has heard *Black Mask* is getting to be "one of the hardest magazines in the country to make" and that he regards this as a compliment. Two months later, good old boy Gene shot off his own kudo. Shaw has created "a fresh and beautifully realistic style in detective stories ... at a time when the standard of such tales [was] almost unbelievably low" (8 November 1931). He expanded his praise with another plug (21 February 1932):

> To appreciate the changes in style worked by Captain Shaw ... one has only to compare a page of *The Virgin Kills* (Whitfield's latest novel) with, say, a page out of any Van Dine novel.
> Van Dine is of the old school. His Philo Vance is a combination of Sherlock Holmes and Raffles.... He carries his Dr. Watson on his shoulder. Artificiality is inherent in the Van Dine novels. You like or dislike as you like or dislike wax roses.

Shaw had spoken fervently along these same lines a few years before in the Asheville, North Carolina, *Sunday Citizen*:

> The day of the Sherlock Holmes ... story is practically ended. Despite the fact that the Fu Manchu and Philo Vance stories have been quite popular, the trend is all toward the serious and realistic presentation in fiction of crime, criminals, the underworld, and police ... as they actually are in real life.
> That this makes for vastly more interesting reading cannot be disputed.... As a result of this change in the character of crime stories has been the production of a new genius in American letters. Yes, genius. [18 August 1929]

Unlike many of his peers who used the blue pencil, Editor Shaw also wrote. His was semi-hardboiled fiction. In 1930 Alfred A. Knopf issued *Derelict*; strangely, this was serialized in *Mask* the following year. But, since he was the chief, Shaw could publish his own work without gainsay. He did so a second time, a three-part serial called "Fugitive" which ran in 1932. That same year Mohawk Press published his *Danger Ahead*, and in 1936 Dodge published *Blood on the Curb*. Frankly, Shaw's fiction was pretty bad and never rivalled that of his own troops.

Ever canny, Shaw made use of the interview to bring him and his rough-paper treasure to the fore. Ed Bodin, on assignment for something called *The Author and Composer* (August 1932), ascends to the eleventh floor of the Ley Building at 587 Madison Avenue, enters Shaw's office, and is at once struck by at least one hundred *Mask* covers framed and on the wall. They gave off "an atmosphere of virility and action," as did Shaw's "grey-streaked hair and mustache" give off a dignified middle-aged appearance. He seemed bigger than his five feet, nine inches.

They get around to discussing the inevitable: How does one break into the charmed circle of *Mask* stars? Bodin proposes that the best way is to read a copy. Shaw:

> Not exactly--but rather study the technique of the ... writers-- not one issue, but a dozen--and suddenly you will feel that fiction punch that tells why their stories are published. You'll find that expert swing and delivery in every story.... Until you can sense it and duplicate it--you are not quite ready to click.

(Little wonder that at one time Erle Stanley Gardner accused Shaw of trying to make every writer write in the same style.)

Bodin pursues. As to the best length, perhaps the short would stand a "better chance"? Yes, Shaw replies. *Mask* doesn't like novelettes over 15,000 words. A new writer's best bet would be "the 6,000 word story, or a little less."

There you are! The prescription!

I will wager that Shaw's greatest moment came when a biographical profile on Dr. Abraham S.W. Rosenbach (1876-1952), eminent book collector, book dealer, and bibliophile, appeared in the press sometime in mid-1933. After considering his fabled and fabulous dealings--e.g., a Gutenberg Bible, Shakespeare First Folios, etc.--in the book world, the conversation veers to detective fiction and Sherlock Holmes.

Says Rosenbach (in *Arkansas Gazette Magazine*):

> He was a marvel of course; but I also love the crime stories that are being written now. What's your favorite detective magazine? I'll tell you what mine is. I get a copy every month the minute it appears on the newsstand. The last number has a corking story. I'll give it to you.

Guess what it was. The July 1933 issue of *Black Mask*! This unexpected bit of bravo was reprinted in newspapers in Los Angeles, Yonkers, New York, and Waterbury, Connecticut, to name a few.[3]

Well, enough already yet. An editor in those days--in these days, too--has to hustle up his customers. Joseph Thompson Shaw was an editorial hustler. He *hustled*. The magazine, sad to say, was nowhere near the same after his departure with the November 1936 issue. Many of his crew left with him. Succeeding editors were generally faceless, even anonymous, and, although there were some very good contributors, none had the talent of a Hammett, a Whitfield, a Chandler, or a Paul Cain.[4]

---

[1] The history of ownership is too complicated to detail here. Dr. Richard Layman has in his possession a xerox copy, and he used the Scrapbook sparingly in his *Shadow Man: The Life of Dashiell Hammett*. To him I owe many thanks for making it available to me.

[2] Marcus Duffield, "The Pulps: Day Dreams for the Masses," *Vanity Fair*, June 1933, pp. 26-27, 51.

[3] The profile appears to have made use of another feature on Dr. Rosenbach, viz., "Merchant to Collectors," *Fortune* 5 (April 1932), 60, 69, 114, 116, 119. However, this version does not have the *Mask* gimmick.

[4] Whether or not *all* the credit should go to Shaw for the development of the *Black Mask* style I have discussed elsewhere; see "*The Black Mask*," *Mystery* 2 (January 1981), 51-53, 59, and "Cap Shaw and His 'Great and Regular Fellows': The Making of *The Hard-Boiled Omnibus*, 1945-1946," *Clues* 2 (Fall/Winter 1981), 143-152.

Detection by Other Means

By Bob Sampson

The manuscript that arrived on the editor's desk one day in 1911 was evidentally titled by amateurs. "Semi-Dual" it was headed, a collaboration between J.U. Giesy and J.B. Smith. As the editor later remarked, "the contents and their nature had never greeted editorial eyes before. Here was a story different...."
The novel, rechristened "The Occult Detector," was published as a three-part serial in *Cavalier* from February 17 through March 2, 1912. Immediately it was followed by a second serial, "The Significance of the High 'D'" (also in three parts, from March 9 through March 23).
So began the fictional career of Prince Abduel Omar of Teheran, Persia, an astrologer, mystic, telepathist, and practical psychologist. Transplanted to America, he practiced his profession from before the first World War into the heart of the Depression. It was a long run over sociologically broken ground.
Prince Omar was more familiarly known as Semi-Dual, an atrocity of a name. It reflects, or was supposed to reflect, his habit of solving criminal problems by a "dual solution--one material for material minds--the other occult, for those who cared to sense a deeper something back of the philosophic lessons interwoven in the narrative."
With dreadful impartiality, the authors referred to him as Semi-Dual, Dual, or Semi. Not even that dimmed his popularity. For twenty-three years, his adventures appeared in the pulp magazines: six serials and two novelettes in *Cavalier* (1912-1913); ten serials and one novelette in *All-Story Weekly* (1914-1920); four novelettes in *People's Magazine* (1917-1918); one novelette in *Top Notch* (July 1, 1918); and eight serials in *Argosy All-Story Weekly* and *Argosy* (1920-1924).
As far as is known, the character never appeared in hard covers, although the equivalent of more than twenty-four books received magazine publication. Taken all together. it is an imposing narrative mass.
Both Giesy and Smith contributed substantially to the pulps during the 'teens and 'twenties under their own signatures or in collaboration with others. Giesy (1877-1947) was a practicing physician in Salt Lake City (another of the writing doctors). He held a number of official posts, including Assistant City Physician, Assistant County Physician, and Acting Police Surgeon. Junius Smith was born in Salt Lake

City in 1883. His grandfather was a brother of Joseph Smith, founder of the Mormon Church. An attorney by profession, Smith practiced in Salt Lake City until 1944. During the early lean years he wrote extensively for the pulps, with Giesy and without. Both men were Fellows of the American Academy of Astrologicians, which probably explains the depth of Dual's technical explanations. These leave you vibrating with the infinite hours later.

Above all, Dual is an astrologer--as well as an exponent "of many other esoteric angles of thought and the application of higher laws of force." In his world, astrology is not merely an amusement filling five inches of daily newspaper space. It is a technique for predicting the interaction of personalities and calculating their subsequent actions. All he needs to begin is the specific birth date--month, day, year, and, if possible, the time. From this information he casts the horoscope--an intensely mathematical process which would clearly benefit from the availability of computer time. He can predict not only actions but an individual's movements at the other side of the world.

> If we know which planet represents the thing we seek, and which planets stand as symbols for themselves,... the time and place when these planets will come to conjunction will indicate the time and place when the various actors in the human drama representative of those planets will meet.... By constant checking of planetary positions, I am enabled to determine that point upon the earth's surface which is indicated by the latitudes and longitudes and declinations of the various planets involved. And as the planets themselves shift in the zodiac, so must I constantly check and recheck, to follow their wanderings in the heavens. ("The Compass in the Sky," *People's Magazine*, May 1917.)

The paperwork is staggering. It involves masses of detailed calculations, a tangle of lines and symbols, an arabesque of astrological equations--"a blending of Old World superstition and modern mathematical precision" is the way the series narrator explains it.

Shocking as it may be to you materialistic, scoffing Americans, to whom nothing is sacred but the Almighty Dollar--shocking as it may seem, Dual is continuously correct. Once that horoscope is cast, then out the future ravels. His accuracy is appaling. In this wicked world, it is so easy to forget that there is such a thing as perfection.

Not that we are nose to nose, here, with predestination, that comfortable excuse for doing your will. Not at all. At various crisis points each individual must make decisions determining his spiritual health. Whether a good decision alters planetary orbits, or a bad one causes Pluto to bump Venus, is outside the scope of these comments.

Just why Dual involves himself in all this labor is not explained. A considerable amount of his time is spent saving women from the toils of evil, and, given that as a hobby, you can see why his days are full:

> Woman is the keeper, the guardian of the flame of life, itself--the worker, in the workshop of the world, whose work is new life. Woman is the priestess in the temple of regeneration. Therefore

... woman should be guarded and kept pure that her life may flow unsullied to the generations to come. ("Compass in the Sky")

The assumption that Woman has some worldly function other than serving as corporation president is now unfashionable. But it's interesting to see how they thought back in 1917.
At any rate, nothing galvanizes Dual to action more rapidly than some young guardian of the flame of life hovering over a pit full of sin.
In addition to defending women, his other major function is to redress evil's balance in the world. In early stories, he several times is able to save the world from disasterous consequences. Later he battles major forces seeking to enshrine the Devil. Still later, when the story scope has contracted, he will be instrumental in crushing gangsters' elaborate plots.
Primarily, Semi-Dual is concerned with people. He will make every effort to save them from crime, or from themselves. He provides the opportunity; they do the saving themselves.
Dual is reasonably accessible. To reach him, go to the Urania Building and ride the elevator to the twentieth floor. From there, walk up the massy bronze and marble staircase leading to the roof.
You exit into a garden, a place of shrubs and blooming bushes. Beds of flowers glow. A fountain plays over lily pads, and goldfish slide slowly in the light. Overhead arcs a roof of green-yellow glass, restraining winter.
At the garden's center bulks a white cube tower. A path leads from this back through the garden to the fancy staircase.
As you enter the garden from the stairs you step on a metal plate. This is inlaid with colored glass, reading "Pause and consider. O stranger: for he who cometh against me with evil intent, shall live to rue it, until the uttermost part of his debt shall have been paid; yet he who cometh in peace, and with a pure heart, shall surely find that which he shall seek."
Pressure on the plate causes a chime of bells in the tower --"soft, mellow as temple bells in the shrine of some half-forgotten god," the authors remark, enthusiastically.
At the tower, Henri (Dual's companion and servant) escorts guests across a reception room decorated in shades of brown and into the office.
It is a large room crammed with Persian delights: a glorious rug, an ancient bronze Venus, life-size, converted prosaically to a clock-lamp (the light glows from the golden apple in her hand, a splendid example of Persian Kitsch). Venus looms beside a massive desk loaded with papers.
Behind it, Semi-Dual.
He is a large man, leonine of head, powerfully built. Assurance and competence radiate from him, an almost visible outpouring of personality. His features are calm, strong, well-formed. The nose is strongly bridged, rather hooked. His eyes are deep gray, the color signifying his position as a lead fictional character. He wears a close-cropped beard.
(The whole description is hero as demi-god. Dual is an early example of that physical-mental excellence which would reassert itself in 1933 in the *Doc Savage Magazine*--and in all those other hundreds of handsome, powerful, wealthy geniuses who chose pulp fiction as a way of life.)
Unlike most characters, Dual wears white robes bordered by

purple. He is the son of a Persian noble and a Russian princess. That blood fusion produced an individual disconcertingly omniscient, in the manner of a tall Nick Carter. His personal wealth, his command of languages, his technical expertise, and, above all, the deference accorded him by the characters, are shining realizations of those wishes meandering hazily in the reader's secret heart.

Dual's interface with the outer, material world is on the seventh floor of the Uranus Building--the firm of "Glace and Bryce, Private Investigators." A private line connects them with the white tower. Dual was largely responsible for the formation of this agency and it stands constantly ready to aid him.

James Bryce, retired Inspector of Police, is half the firm. A substantial, tough old-timer, he is heavy-set, wears a stubby brown mustache, and grinds away at a black cigar. He is neither stupid nor incompetent. Behind him is a life of successful police investigation in big-city law enforcement. He is hard-nosed, discerning, has city-wide contacts.

Gordon Glace, narrator of the stories, is younger than Bryce. Solidly built and competent, he was formerly a reporter on the *Record* (whose editor first named Dual "The Occult Detector"). While a reporter, Glace met Dual, assisted him in certain early cases to clean up "police tangles." At Dual's suggestion, Glace changed his vocation to detective. He is married to the charming Connie, met in an early novel.

These three characters and Dual are the continuing core of the series. Other minor characters appear at intervals, but the regulars provide the continuing fram about which Dual's enchantments twine.

From first to last, the series covered such major astonishments as World War I, Prohibition and the Jazz Age, and the Depression. Distinctive times. They flavored the prose. The earliest stories move with crisp tension. They are told by Glace, at that time an unmarried reporter who consults with his strange, predictive friend. The action is usually seen through Glace's eyes. His solo flights into peril are monitored mysteriously from afar by Dual, hovering off the edge of the page, peering in. "The House of the Ego" (*Cavalier*, three-part serial, September 20 through October 4, 1913) tells of a young woman who wishes to do good, good, good. She has fallen into the talons of Bhutia, a crooked swami. Bhutia operates a mansion of instruction (The House of the Ego) which is filled with thin-witted seekers of Mystic Symbols and Occult Meanings, all slowly bleeding into the swami's bank account.

Glace insinuates himself into the house as a student of the swami's lore. The mansion is straight out of Nick Carter --or perhaps Old Cap Collier. It is a house within a house, the space between filled with secret passages, secret stairs, secret levers, secret switches. Extra added attractions also include magnetic door locks, secret panel controls, mystic hangings, a deadly cobra, a pair of evil schemers, and a fine death plot against Glace, whose connection with that noted cop, Bryce, has been discovered.

It hardly seems possible that Glace can save either the girl or himself.

But the swami has reckoned without Semi-Dual ....

"The Compass in the Sky" *People's Magazine*, May 1917) is

one of those lavishly detailed adventure stories stamped by
the African romances of H. Rider Haggard. Little seems drawn
from the works of Edgar Rice Burroughs, although the story includes a beautiful girl abducted and carried across Africa, a
situation Burroughs had already exploited lavishly.
   The girl is Madeleine Lemaire, daughter of the French Commander at Fort Grampel. Alas for her. She is lusted after by
Lt. Jean Marsal. He lusts also for German gold and has stolen
important papers which will precipitate an international incident if the Germans get them. Off heads Marsal across
Africa, papers under his coat, Madeleine tied to an adjacent
horse.
   In 1917 it was not proper for a young lady to accompany a
man across the trackless veldt. Sleeping in his tent, un-
chaperoned--my dear, I could die with shame! This revolting
state of affairs is glossed over by Madeleine's flat statement
that, if he lays a finger-tip on her, she will kill herself.
That defers, if it does not quench, Marsal's zealous ardor.
He doubles his efforts to seduce her with smiles and winning
words. And so onward they ride, a decidedly uncomfortable
pair, as ....
   ... across the seas, in the Urania Building, Semi-Dual
summons Glace telepathically. ("You ought to get your brains
insulated," growls Bryce.) They are leaving immediately for
Paris. The French people need them. Poor Connie is left to
her cold, solitary dinner, and off they go to Paris, where the
Chief of Police and the Head of the French Secret Service ask
Dual's aid in averting world catastrophe.
   Matters are hardly so grave. The stolen papers reveal a
French scheme for extending their influence in Morocco, repre-
hensible but hardly disasterous. But you know how those
Frenchmen carry on.
   Dual dazzles them all by displaying knowledge that he
could not possibly have, right down to the fact that Marsal
has stolen the girl. As he says, in a matter-of-fact voice,

   each man has some planetary force which governs the thing we call
   destiny. If one knows the ruling sign and the planet and the
   planetary influence in operation at a certain time, one may fore-
   cast what the future may hold.... It is no more than the application of a proved and existing natural law, based on the inter-
   changing moves of magnetic force between star and star.

   Even in this 1917 astrological statement, the occult is no
more than an expression of natural law. It is not magic but
rational science, dressed in white and purple robes.
   Now begins one of those splendid trips across the face of
the world that the pulps did so well: from Paris to Algiers,
by train to Tunis. There Glace infiltrates a small group of
German agents, who accept him rather more readily than they
would do in the real world. Thence to Khartoum.
   At this famous place, Dual shows up in the company of a
big tough native named Shemba. The lead German is captured,
tied, and tossed into a boat before he can gasp "Vaterland."
Onward the travelers go, up the Nile to the Lost Land of Ophir.
Dual checks planetary progress by the day, calculating, calculating. The German sweats. Glace makes notes for the book
he will write.
   According to the stars, they will intercept Marsal and

Madeleine up ahead. But something is awry--the planets diverge. Madeleine has escaped, taking refuge in a vast ruined city, a colossal wreck of gigantic walls and vast brooding avenues and frowning ruins, the immense temple glimmering evily in the fading light.

Down among the catacombs, in a cavern decoratively stocked with skeletons, hids the girl, hardly to be extracted even by astrology. By this time, Dual and company have captured Marsal. As they bring Madeleine up away from the skeletons, the evil Frenchman escapes with a triumphant cry.

Shemba shoots him dead, then turns his attention to repelling Marsal's minions, now shrieking down upon them.

Even this Dual has foreseen. Per his instructions given weeks before, Algerian troops arrive, just at that instant, and with a blast of rifle fire obliterate all final traces of evil. The story ends in a spasm of fierce joy--virginity has been preserved, the Kaiser checked, French imperialism unfettered, and astrology, the glorious science, vindicated. Up the planets.

After the conclusion of the First World War, this positive tone falters and is greatly subdued. The serious literature of the period showed distinct tendencies to sever all connections with former generations and their works. It was not that these connections were evil in themselves, but that spokesmen of the previous generation had been so conspicuously wrong in so many things. Men who have been launched on frontal attacks against massed machine guns, entrenched and sited in depth, are not apt, afterward, to applaud the wisdom of their leaders.

The war introduced all manner of neurotic symptoms into fiction. There was general disillusionment with everything that one might be illusioned with. There was also a calculated search for gratification, personal and immediate, and a vehement denial that contemporary social structures remained relevant. There were equally strong feelings that some sort of conspiracy lay at the root of it all.

Some blamed the Jews, some the munitions makers, or the Wall Street capitalists, or the Huns, or sinister plotters lurking within the British Empire. The paranoic whimperings were further reinforced by a sharp economic depression following the cut-back of government contracts at the end of the war.

Even the studied optimism of popular fiction wavered. The story of adventure tended, more frequently, to become a story of single struggle against shapeless evil, concealed and vastly powerful, sitting erect in the darkness, black teeth slimed, and waiting.

Which is neurosis. And which (to shrink our horizons to the issue at hand) may possibly explain certain elements in the Semi-Dual novels published during 1918-1921.

At first you notice little change. "The Black Butterfly" (four-part serial in *All-Story Weekly*, September 14 through October 5, 1918) seems as barren of clues as some of Nero Wolfe's cases, years later. A celebrated beauty is found murdered, dressed in the costume of a black butterfly. Upon this enigma the detectives batter in vain, until Dual reveals the truth using psychometry (or perhaps manipulating psychology) and the interpretation of paintings by the insane.

The post-war emotional sickness begins showing itself

through the next serials. These form a series within the
Semi-Dual series and pit Dual and his friends against the
Black Brotherhood, representatives of the Devil on earth,
worshipers of Erlik, Commander of the Hosts of All Evil.
By embracing evil, the Brotherhood has relinquished personal souls. Death is a total stop for them; they die and
cease to exist. Very disagreeable. Their battle with Dual
gradually escalates through the serials, employing ever more
extraordinary devices--psychic bombs, telepathic spying, mass
hypnotism, and what would pass for out-and-out magic if it
weren't so deftly explained.
    The sequence of four serials, all of which were published
in *All-Story Weekly*, begins with "The Ivory Pipe" (three parts,
September 20 through October 4, 1919). Next followed "House
of the Hundred Lights" (three parts, May 22 through June 5,
1920); then "Black and White" (four parts, October 2 through
October 23, 1920); and finally "Wolfe of Erlik" (four parts,
October 22 through November 12, 1921).
    By "Black and White," Dual has so interferred with the
Brotherhood that it sends an assassin after him. She is Lotis
Popoff, daughter of a "Red" who committed suicide in the previous story. Lotis comes against Dual with evil in her heart
and, as his glass-inlaid plate promised, she lives to rue it.
He immediately captures her, then hypnotizes her, hoping
to save her soul (for she has performed no overt evil deed and
can still be saved). The Leader of the Brotherhood, a fiend
named Otho Khan, now turns all his skill to destroying both
Lotis and Dual, and our hero has a busy time of it keeping the
girl alive; either her vital energies are being drained away
or she is attempting to leap from the top of the Urania Building. Always something.
    Echoes of the recent war, weirdly reshaped by the general
atmosphere of psychic-occult wonder, bang and rattle within
the action. Dual is attacked by Otho's psychic bomb. This
appears as a sort of singularity in the air, amazing Glace.
The bomb allows remote reading of minds and has the added advantage of exploding with immense violence, exactly like the
Western Front.
    That scheme is foiled without much trouble. Then Otho
begins a major attack. Dual's rooftop is assailed by three
men. Smoke bombs are exploded and through the haze appear two
killers disguised as firemen. Their assignment is to chop
Dual up with fire axes.
    The effort fails. Dual gestures hypnotically in the manner of Mandrake the Majician, causing the axes to writhe into
giant snakes. The hit men stand transfixed. The third man,
Otho's second-in command, is driven from the scene by Lotis,
who jets fire at him from her dagger.
    This is the action climax of the novel. It is a rather
trifling affair. Four long serial parts build up to this
shrunken climax; it is a Fourth of July celebration climaxed
by a single firecracker. "Black and White" barely waddles
along, laden by tons of description and talk. Particularly
talk. Everyone jabbers at everyone else: Dual soothes Lotis,
Lotis is desperate, the police talk with Bryce, Bryce talks
with the police, everyone talks apprehensively and peers over
his shoulder. How slowly this action story drags. What Giesy
and Smith intended was to show all the action occuring on a
spiritual level, only occasionally translating into action in

the material world.
It drags.
"Wolf of Erlik" is a trifle busier and contains many good scenes, most of them involving Lotis. She is married now, fighting at Dual's side to smash the power of the Brotherhood. This organization has gathered unto itself many voodoo worshippers. They are concealed in a cave, and there they chant and sweat, while Otho, sloshing with evil, schemes and snarls.
The fight between Dual and Otho is excessively astral. It employs "thoughts--the dynamic lances and swords and spears of the human mind."
Illusion is meant. Lotis fights a yowling mob of voodooers--on this occasion, Otho has descended to physical violence--and drives the rascals off by changing yarn bits from her knitting into flaming serpents. When you are a voodoo worshiper, this transformation violently unsettles your mind. It's mass hypnotism, Glace assumes, or conscious thought projection. It's wonderful.
Afterward, Lotis allows Dual to send her astral form out and away to Otho's cave. There she spies on his plans and reads his lieutenant's mind and has a perfectly splendid time, a sort of living psychic spy satellite.
Through all these stories, each action has a double meaning. Every event is swathed in mumbo jumbo, until you feel the walls begin to move around you. Afterward, a perfectly rational explanation is given. Thus, in "Black and White," Lotis and knife appear mysteriously and get a great build-up as the striking force of Otho appearing from nowhere. Sensation. Later it develops that she was smuggled up in the elevator, causing the wonder to reel and go dim. In "Erlik," a major psychic attack is launched against Dual, presumably by concentrating all those voodoo minds. Then things turn around. We learn that everyone was uneasy, not because of focused minds but because the ceaseless pounding of drums was bothering them. Dual explanations all; all forced.
Two new characters have been added to the cast. Inspector Johnson, City Police, has become the series' official contact with the Law. And Danny Quinn, the office boy for Glace & Bryce, has developed sufficient characteristics to begin carrying plot responsibility. A former newsboy, red-headed and clever as all newsboys are, he matures through the rest of the series, and by "The Ledger of Life" (1934) he is a full operative in the firm.
After "Erlik" the series swings from post-war gloom and devil plotters to the more homey fields of the gangster. "The Opposing Venus" (*Argosy All-Story Weekly*, four parts, October 13 through November 3, 1923) concerns a mob-based blackmail ring that is not above using women to ensnare men. Dual predicts and manipulates from afar, laboring to save a girl far gone in sin--but not too far gone. At the end, Glace and Johnson race about the city while the whole criminal plot comes unglued. Gangsters have livened up the story. There is even a running shoot-out with the mastermind, who dies by his own hand. Dual rarely participates directly in these exciting adventures; he appears in the final chapter to speak fat paragraphs of comfort and spiritual solace: "So in the end is the measure of a man's sin returned upon him, to crush him into nothingness. For it is written that as one soweth so shall one inevitably reap, and he who sows the wind shall reap the

whirlwind, and he who sows good deeds shall reap--peace."
   For those interested in the technical side of astrology, let it be known that Dual identified the mind behind the blackmail ring by casting his horoscope (after much delay in securing his birth data) and discovering conclusively that only this one fellow, of all the participants, had exactly the right characteristics to qualify as head of the ring.
   For after all, "All force is one--and matter but its expression in a concrete way." Even so.
   "The Green Goddess" (*Argosy*, January 31 through March 7, 1931) is a six-part serial concerning the strange events at the night club The Green Goddess, a dope distribution center and gangster hideout. "Oriental mystery and the horrors of a hasheesh-maddened mind ... shroud the disappearance of an American heiress in a night club." So advises *Argosy*'s editor, shaking with excitement. Matters in the serial quickly become so frantic that Dual, himself, makes a public appearance in his own identity, Prince Abdul Omar, all splendid in robes and full turban with giant ruby, dazzling the patrons of The Green Goddess. The story was illustrated by John McNeil, who did all those interiors for the Land of Oz books.
   "The Ledger of Life" (*Argosy*, four-part serial, June 30 through July 21, 1934) was published almost three and a half years after "The Green Goddess." This case also involves a night club. A woman is murdered there under strange circumstances. She was a blackmailer and was surrounded by people who wished to do her in. Almost as many sinister characters are involved in the mystery as appear in a Raymond Chandler novel, all tough and slangy and linked one to the other like urban cockleburrs. Crooked real estate deals are disclosed, and fresh bodies, and one-way rides in closed riding cars in the grand Chicago style. Glace, Bryce, and Inspector Johnson team up and spend time, gasoline, and the reader's patience driving earnestly about. Semi-Dual spends a lot of time offstage, considering that he's the lead character, but his hand is everywhere.
   The finale is one of those ancient Craig Kennedy seances where all the characters gather to listen to the lead detective explain what all the serial parts have been about. Dual does so, thus justifying inclusion of the story in his series.
   The case ends with gunfire (off scene), suggesting that mystic trappings needed to be jazzed up with something more hearty by 1934. As the echoes die away, Dual rises impressively: "It is ended. From the Court of Cosmic Justice there is no appeal."
   The mastermind was a positively snaky lawyer, you see, so the remark is appropriate.
   Dual now approaches the girl of this final adventure. She has been through the storm and, glorified, has found her man. As she clutches him fiercely, Dual stands over them and, in a ringing voice, pronounces his final words: "Daughter of Life, you have served. The Balance is in your favor. It brings you your reward."
   You can distinctly hear the authors pant as they struggle to pump mystic overtones into a gun-blazing crook story.

   The Semi-Dual series stretches across more than twenty years. When it began in 1912, spiritualism sought to communicate with the dead by solemn inanities; when the series ended, the New Deal, in its own occult way, struggled to communicate with a dead economy. Between these points flowed the adventures of Semi-Dual, an extended series that was at least as rational as the world around it. Like any other successful series, it changed with the times. The occult detective coped with hateful Germans during the First World War and with the forces of Erlik immediately afterward, the Devil being the cause of post-war distress. When the gangster and the bootlegger superseded the Devil's legions, the series shifted adversaries and continued the good fight.

Whether the theme was adventure in foreign lands or thought combat or gangster plots, the Semi-Dual series produced its own distinctive interpretations of the world. It emphatically presented a universe operating to laws misunderstood or ignored, modified by tides of significant force never sensed by the players in reality. This is a coherent world, shockingly close but inaccessible to few other than Persian mystics. Whatever your niggling prejudices against the bright white truths of astrology, they must fall silent before the achievements of Prince Abdul Omar. His successes speak for themselves.

Tremble unbelievers and come in peace, or Mars will prod Jupiter and you will long regret your cynical ways.

A CHECKLIST OF SEMI-DUAL STORIES

(Note: This list was originally prepared by William J. Clark and published in his Semi-Dual article, "The Occult Detector by J.B. Giesy and Junius B. Smith," in *Xenophile* No. 17, September 1975, p. 55. The format of Mr. Clark's list has been modified.)

1912
"The Occult Detector," *The Cavalier*, serialized February 17, 24, March 2.
"The Significance of the High 'D'," *The Cavalier*, serialized March 9, 16, 23.
"The Wistaria Scarf," *The Cavalier*, serialized June 1, 8, 15.
"The Purple Light," *The Cavalier*, serialized October 5, 12, 19.

1913
"The Master Mind," *The Cavalier*, novelette, January 25.
"Rubies of Doom," *The Cavalier*, serialized July 5, 12.
"The House of the Ego," *The Cavalier*, serialized September 20, 27, October 4.
"The Ghost of a Name," *The Cavalier*, novelette, December 20.

1914
"The Curse of Quetzal," *All-Story Magazine*, novelette, November 28.

1915
"The Web of Destiny," *All-Story Weekly*, serialized March 20, 27.
"Snared," *All-Story Weekly*, serialized December 11, 18, 25.

1916
"Box 991," *All-Story Weekly*, serialized June 3, 10, 17.

1917
"The Killer," *All-Story Weekly*, serialized April 7, 14, 21, 28.

"The Compass in the Sky," *The People's Magazine*, novelette, May.
"The Unknown Quantity," *All-Story Weekly*, serialized August 25, September 1, 8.
"Solomon's Decision," *All-Story Weekly*, serialized December 1, 8, 15.

1918
"The Storehouse of Past Events," *People's Favorite Magazine*, novel, February 10.
"The Moving Shadow," *People's Favorite Magazine*, novelette, June 10.
"The Stars Were Looking," *Top-Notch Magazine*, believed to be a novelette, July 1.
"The Black Butterfly," *All-Story Weekly*, serialized September 14, 21, 28, October 5.
"The Trail in the Dust," *People's Favorite Magazine*, novel, October 25.

1919
"Stars of Evil," *All-Story Weekly*, serialized January 25, February 1, 8.
"The Ivory Pipe," *All-Story Weekly*, serialized September 20, 27, October 4.

1920
"House of the Hundred Lights," *All-Story Weekly*, serialized May 22, 29, June 5, 12.
"Black and White," *Argosy All-Story Weekly*, serialized October 2, 9, 16, 23.

1921
"Wolf of Erlik," *Argosy All-Story Weekly*, October 22, 29, November 5, 12.

1923
"The Opposing Venus," *Argosy All-Story Weekly*, serialized October 13, 20, 27, November 3.

1924
"Poor Little Pigeon," *Argosy All-Story Weekly*, serialized August 9, 16, 23, 30, September 6, 13.

1926
"The House of Invisible Bondage," *Argosy All-Story Weekly*, serialized September 18, 25, October 2, 9.

1929
"The Woolly Dog," *Argosy All-Story Weekly*, serialized March 23, 30, April 6, 13.

1931
"The Green Goddess," *Argosy*, serialized January 31, February 7, 14, 21, 28, March 7.

1934
"The Ledger of Life," *Argosy*, serialized June 30, July 7, 14, 21.

Joe Orton's and Tom Stoppard's Burlesques of the Detective Genre

By Earl F. Bargainnier

There is a long tradition of burlesques and parodies of the detective genre, stretching back at least to W.S. Gilbert's *A Sensational Novel*, a play produced in 1871. Plays, poems, short stories and even novels have played with and mocked the conventions and cliches of the form. The Sherlock Holmes stories have received more of such treatment than any other group, a natural phenomenon because of their fame and popularity, but every type of detective story has been burlesqued. (To be pedantic, a parody mocks a specific work, whereas a burlesque mocks a genre or type. The latter is most often in dramatic form; when it is not, it is generally just described as satire.) To the long list of writers--among whom are Ronald Knox, Stephen Leacock, Ogden Nash, and S.J. Perelman-- who have delighted in the comic possibilities of detective fiction have recently been added the names of two of the most significant of post-modernist British dramatists: Joe Orton (1933-1967) and Tom Stoppard (born 1937).
In his brief life Orton wrote seven plays (Joe Orton, *The Complete Plays* [New York: Grove Press, 1982]). They earned him the epithet "the master farceur of his age" and comparison to Oscar Wilde as a contributor to British comedy. His death could easily form the basis of a crime novel: he was bludgeoned to death with a hammer by his long-time male lover Kenneth Halliwell, who then committed suicide by swallowing twenty-two sleeping pills. Three of his plays deal with crime in a farcical or absurdist manner. *What the Butler Saw*, produced in 1969, sounds like the title of a detective story; instead, it is a manic play set in a mental clinic, and no butler ever appears. However, one of the characters is Sergeant Match, a pompous, bungling police officer attempting to locate Winston Churchill's missing male organ (anything is possible in an Orton play!). *Entertaining Mr. Sloan* (1964) is a farcical thriller, in which the handsome young hood Sloan commits two murders, but he is protected by a middle-aged brother and sister, for sexual reasons, even though the second victim is their father. The play turns the concepts of family, criminality, and justice upside-down, ending with the brother and sister agreeing to share Sloan's sexual attractions, each having him for six months. (The acclaimed 1981 Cheery Lane Theatre production of the play in New York starred Maxwell Caulfield, the new teen idol of the film *Grease II*, as Sloan.)

Both of these plays use the motif of the disruptive intruder, but for satire rather than terror.
Most deliberately burlesque is Orton's *Loot* (1966). Like most farcical plots, that of *Loot* loses its impact in summary. Suffice it to say, there is a murder and an unrelated robbery before the play opens; the action consists of attempts to hide the "loot" in the corpse's coffin and to hide the body elsewhere. However, these efforts are foiled by the arrival of the principal burlesque character, Inspector Truscott of Scotland Yard. Truscott seems to be influenced by J.B. Priestley's *An Inspector Calls* (1945), which was filmed in 1954 with Alastair Sim as the omniscient, mysterious inspector. Orton surely saw this major British film, and memories of it must have played a part in his characterization of Truscott. However, where the inspector of Priestley's play is a supernatural being--if you will, an angel--sent to reveal to people their true natures, Orton's Truscott is a "fascist bully," whose omniscience serves only a moribund establishment, if even that. In his first appearances, he denies being a police officer, claiming to be an official from the water board, which he makes sound omnipotent. When he finally reveals his identity, he does so with a flourish, a grotesquely burlesque flourish:

> TRUSCOTT. You have before you a man who is quite a personage in his way--Truscott of the Yard. Have you never heard of Truscott? The man who tracked down the limbless girl killer? Or was that sensation before your time?
> HAL. Who would kill a limbless girl?
> TRUSCOTT. She was the killer.
> HAL. How did she do it if she was limbless?
> TRUSCOTT. I'm not prepared to answer that question to anyone outside the profession. We don't want a carbon-copy murder on our hands.

As a great detective, he states that he conducts his cases "under an assumed voice and I am a master of disguise (*He takes off his hat.*) You see--a complete transformation." At the same time, he can haggle over the amount of an offered bribe and be utterly sadistic. After knocking a man to the floor, he says, "Under any other political system I'd have you on the floor in tears." To another he says, "If I ever hear you accuse the police of using violence on a prisoner in custody again, I'll take you down to the station and beat the eyes out of your head."
That Truscott is not just an isolated example of the policeman as sadist, but is working with, if not for, the powers that control society is evident in the following passage of dialogue:

> FAY. You must prove me guilty. That is the law.
> TRUSCOTT. You know nothing of the law. I know nothing of the law. That makes us equal in the sight of the law.
> FAY. I'm innocent till I'm proved guilty. This is a free country. The law is impartial.
> TRUSCOTT. Who's been filling your head with that rubbish? ...
> FAY. Have you no respect for the truth?
> TRUSCOTT. We have a saying under the blue lamp: "Waste time on the truth and you'll be pounding the beat until the day you retire."

FAY (*breaking down*). The British police force used to be run by
men of integrity.
TRUSCOTT. That is a mistake which has been rectified.

Such satire of the system is far from funny when taken out of
context, but within the play it becomes another of Orton's
jibes at detectival omniscience and what he sees as the hollow-
ness behind it. The same is true of Truscott's cavalier view
of evidence:

TRUSCOTT. And here—(*Triumphantly he takes a sheet of paper from
his pocket.*)—the evidence on which I propose to convict: a
recent specimen of the handwriting of your late wife's nurse.
Identical in every respect.
MACLEAVY (*staring at the sheet of paper*). But this is signed
Queen Victoria.
TRUSCOTT. One of her many aliases.

At the end, Truscott teams with the two robbers and the murderer to gain the loot and frame the innocent father of one of
the robbers. The play's last line is stated by the murderer:
"We must keep up appearances." Altogether, *Loot* is a mordant
and acerbic burlesque of the conventional pipe-smoking Scotland Yard detective of fiction and drama, as well as of the
values of the society that produced and sustains the image of
that conventional type in the minds of most people.
    Somewhat less farcical and more intellectual--but just as
funny--are the plays of Tom Stoppard, Britain's leading dram-
atist of the present generation. Since the success of his
Rosencrantz and Guildersten Are Dead in 1967, he has consistently written witty verbal extravanganzas--such as *Jumpers*
(1972), *Travesties* (1974), *Dirty Linen* (1976), and *Night and
Day* (1978)--which have made him both a critic's favorite and a
popular success. Two of his plays, one major and one minor,
are burlesques of the detective genre--and much else as well.
The minor play is the short *After Magritte* (1971), in which
the detective is Foot of the Yard and his assistant is Police
Constable Holmes. Their comic investigation of the Harris
household is circular with Foot finally being revealed as the
mysterious one-legged man seen about (a probable reference to
Jonathan Small of *The Sign of the Four*): in running to move
his illegally parked car outside his house, he had accidentally
put both of his legs into one leg of his pajamas. The title
is a pun on the names of the surreal painter Magritte and
Simenon's Maigret.
    A much more significant work is *The Real Inspector Hound*
(1968), which has already become a modern comic classic. Its
blend of wit, burlesque of detective fiction and drama, and
the theme of uncertainty, of the unreliability of the mind to
discover truth because of ever shifting perspectives, which
undercuts the basis of the detective genre, are presented as a
play within a play. The critics Moon and Birdboot watch a
performance of a traditional mystery play until they are drawn
into the action and finally become two of the victims. Their
comments on the performance show their stupidity, for all of
their assumptions are wrong; in a sense, the play is a game,
and they are the losers. One obvious target of the play within a play is Agatha Christie's play *The Mousetrap*, evidenced
by the isolated house (Muldoon Manor, surrounded by desolate

marshes and enclosed by fog, rather than snow), an unexpected guest, an escaped murderer, and, most significantly, the detective as murderer. However, any number of conventions from mystery novels or plays are skewered by Stoppard: radio warnings, entrances and exits by a prominent French window (including one young lady's entrance chasing a tennis ball), a corpse on the stage not discovered until the second act, a husband mysteriously missing for ten years, names such as Felicity Cunningham, Cynthia Muldoon and Mrs. Drudge the maid, a wheelchair-bound Major "who turned up out of the blue from Canada just the other day," a card game with ambiguous comments by the players, an interminable and too-too formal serving of afternoon tea, and various characters saying to others some variation of "I'll kill you."

By the end of the play, four characters are dead, and most of the others have turned into--or out to be--someone else. Major Magnus, the supposed invalid in the wheelchair, is *in toto* the missing Lord Muldoon, the "real" Inspector Hound, and Puckridge, a third-string critic who eliminates Moon and Birdboot. Not only are such changes burlesques of the hidden identities of the detective genre, but they also subvert the belief that reason can determine the truth, for in this plot there is no ultimate truth.

While accomplishing what could be called the destruction of the genre's basis, *The Real Inspector Hound* has great fun at the expense of detective fiction's style or lack of it. Three particular elements of style that are mocked are the exclamations of fear--here combined with wornout conventions-- the presentation of exposition, and long, involved--here incomprehensible--explanations. The first of these is illustrated by the following:

> CYNTHIA: But what are we going to do?
> HOUND (*snatching the phone*): I'll phone the police!
> CYNTHIA: But you are the police!
> HOUND: Thank God I'm here--the lines have been cut!
> CYNTHIA: You mean--?
> HOUND: Yes!--we're on our own, cut off from the world and in grave danger!
> CYNTHIA: You mean--?
> HOUND: Yes!--I think the killer will strike again!
> MAGNUS: You mean--?
> HOUND: Yes! One of us ordinary mortals thrown together by fate and cut off by the elements is the murderer! He must be found --search the house!

Since the plots of mysteries are so often complex, the problem of presenting necessary exposition for intelligibility can be a serious one, and writers sometimes have to resort to clumsy narrative devices. Not so in this play: the characters are only too happy to tell us everything we need to know--and more:

> MRS. DRUDGE (*into phone*): Hello, the drawingroom of Lady Muldoon's country residence one morning in early spring.... I hope nothing is amiss for we, that is Lady Muldoon and her houseguests, are here cut off from the world, including Magnus, the wheelchair-ridden half-brother of her ladyship's husband Lord Albert Muldoon who ten years ago went for a walk on the cliffs

was never seen again.

The critic Moon's comment is "Derivative, of course," and he is answered by Birdboot's "But quite sound." Almost as soon as Mrs. Drudge puts down the phone, a young man enters:

> SIMON: Ah!--hello there! I'm Simon Gascoyne, I hope you don't mind, the door was open so I wandered in. I'm a friend of Lady Muldoon, the lady of the house, having made her acquaintance through a mutual friend, Felicity Cunningham, shortly after moving into this neighborhood just the other day.
> MRS. DRUDGE: I'm Mrs. Drudge. I don't live in but pop in on my bicycle when the weather allows to help in the running of charming though somewhat isolated Muldoon Manor. Judging by the time (*she glances at the clock*) you did well to get here before high water cut us off for all practical purposes from the outside world.
> SIMON: I took the short cut over the cliffs and followed one of the old smugglers' paths through the treacherous swamps that surround this strangely inaccessible house.
> MRS. DRUDGE: Yes, many visitors have remarked on the topographical quirk in the local strata whereby there are no roads leading from the Manor, though there *are* ways of getting *to* it, weather allowing.

The two quite different final explanations, neither of which is correct, are too long to quote, but the Inspector's explanation of the motive can provide some idea of the nonsensical reasoning present:

> HOUND: William Herbert McCoy who as a young man, meeting the madman in the street and being solicited for sixpence for a cup of tea, replied, "Why don't you do a decent day's work, you shifty old bag of horse manure," in Canada all those many years ago.... The madman was a mere boy at the time but he never forgot that moment, and thenceforth carried in his heart the promise to revenge! (*At which point he finds himself standing on top of the corpse. He looks down carefully.*) Is there anything you have forgotten to tell me?

Other examples of deliberate mockery of stylistic solecisms could be given--such as the police combing the swamps for a known madman and shouting through loudspeakers, "Don't be a madman, give yourself up"--but there are simply too many. The entire play is a send-up of the conventions and formulas (and cliches) of the detective genre, and fans of that genre, knowing best what is being burlesqued, should laugh loudest at its satiric absurdities.

It has often been said that parody is the truest form of flattery. The same is true of burlesque, for one cannot mock a literary form unless one has spent time learning its characteristics. Since the detective genre has well-defined formulas and conventions, it is not surprising that it has been chosen so often for parody and burlesque. The deliberately outrageous works of Orton and the intellectually sophisticated ones of Stoppard are recent illustrations of how writers-- while presenting other themes at the same time--have found burlesques of the detective genre a means of structuring works and creating laughter.

Bloody Balaclava

Charlotte MacLeod's Campus Comedy Mysteries

By Jane S. Bakerman

When a crime fiction enthusiast speaks of Balaclava, she is thinking neither of a great battle nor of a knitted woolen helmet. Indeed not. For murder mystery fans, Balaclava means one thing only: Balaclava Agricultural College, the farmer's answer to MIT. Detective story readers visit Balaclava courtesy of Charlotte MacLeod[1] who has, to date, depicted the school in *Rest You Merry* (1978)[2] and *The Luck Runs Out* (1979),[3] sprightly, humorous, traditional whodunits.

All traditional crime stories are organized in the same basic fashion: disorder (usually murder) invades an essentially orderly society; the detective seeks out the source of the disorder, unmasks the villain who is then punished, and thereby order is restored. Proud of its heritage, Balaclava represents, in many ways, the most orderly of ordered societies. It is conservative in its outlook and, naturally, agrarian in its orientation. Most Balaclava faculty members are well-known and respected in their various fields. Professor Enderble, for instance, is esteemed as the author of *How to Live with the Burrowing Animals* and *Never Dam a Beaver*, landmark works. Similarly, Professor Feldster, given to such scholarly activities as reading monographs (for example, "The History of Cream Separation") at meetings of the National Dairymen's Association, has made a "significant contribution to the subject of Butterfat Content" (*Luck*, 154).

Furthermore, *unlike* most contemporary institutions of higher learning, Balaclava is financially stable; the college shares in the royalties from such monetarily successful developments as Professors Shandy and Ames' Balaclava Buster, a highly commercial strain of rutabaga, as well as the proceeds from their Portulaca Purple Passion and the Sprightly Sieglinde, "an extra-fast-sprouting viola" (*Rest*, 19). Sensibly, the college not only provides all its own power from its methane gas plant, the Cookie Works, "run solely on by-products from the digestive process ... of ... the college herds" (*Luck*, 73), but also the school sells its excess power to neighboring homes, and the rates are *not* cheap.

Because of the Cookie Works, Balaclava Agricultural College is able, even in these days of outrageous prices, to sponsor its annual Grand Illumination, an event which also feeds the coffers. The Grand Illumination is an entertainment running from before Christmas through New Year's. Students give up their winter vacations to operate the parking lots, sleigh rides, and the Gingerbread Houses, refreshment stands which sell cider (locally made) and such munchables as Coconut Cowpats (baked on campus). The undergraduates also sculpt giant snowmen, appear with the Eskimo Piemen, a carolling group, and dress up as Santa's helpers to haul visitors around on little sleds. Tours are conducted through Balaclava Crescent, the faculty row whose homes are stunningly decorated for the season--mostly with multitudes of electric lights, all powered by the Cookie Works, all paid for by the householders. "From near and far came tourists to bask in the spectacle and be milked by the lads and lasses of Balaclava.... Pictures appeared in national magazines" (*Rest*, 1-2). The school gains free publicity; the tourists have a good, pricey time; and college and student workers split the proceeds. All very satisfactory.

At first glance, then, Balaclava Agricultural College seems secure, fortunate in its industrious students, its distinguished faculty, its strong financial base. But though Balaclava is bucolic, it is not Edenic; the appearance of order is sometimes misleading, cloaking acts of theft, adultery, and even murder, that gravest of disorders which disrupt orderly societies. It is these moments which MacLeod depicts in her campus comedy mysteries.

Rest You Merry centers around the murders of two rather unpleasant, meddling Balaclava employees. *The Luck Runs Out* treats the armed robbery of a nearby silver-crafting establishment, the murder of Flackley the Farrier, long a college mainstay, *and* the pignapping of Belinda of Balaclava! Readers must not mistake this third crime as a minor one, as MacLeod makes clear:

> Belinda is no ordinary sow. She is a vital link in a chain of genetic experiments which ... our animal husbandry department has been conducting over a period of almost thirty years and is almost due to farrow. The piglets she produces, it is hoped, will constitute a major step forward in pig breeding. Therefore, while her value in money alone is not inconsiderable, her importance to the science of swine breeding may be almost incalculable. (*Luck*, 59-60)

Finance, progress, and murder, it would seem, often go hand in hand at BAC.

Both novels focus on campus festivals; the first takes place during the Grand Illumination, and the second occurs during preparations for the Annual Competition of the Balaclava County Draft Horse Association, thus enabling MacLeod to make the most of her setting and to treat the college as an actual character in her tales. By stressing Balaclava, by raising the institution to the role of character, MacLeod is ringing a nice change on a major trend in mystery/detective fiction, the exploitation of a specialized setting to lend interest and complication to the plots. In the tradition of Emma Lathen, whose humorous mystery novels depict, debunk, and exploit the American banking-investment community, MacLeod is going yet one step further. The Balaclava novels are actually comedies of manners, stories in which the habits, behavior patterns, and mores of a specific, recognizable subculture are subjected to close, ironic scrutiny.

Much of the literary critic's joy in the Balaclava bunch

arises from the fun of watching a form, the comedy of manners, which usually treats a very urbane, polished, mannered social group, being applied to the homespun environs of an Ag-school. But here, in a really clever stroke, the author has it both ways: true, the Balaclava staff and students are in one sense rustics, but they are also either polished professionals or pre-professionals undergoing the polishing process. They know what they are doing and are doing it well, *even if* their professional activities sometimes seem arcane to the outsider. Spending one's energies writing carefully crafted papers for audiences of fellow aficionados--is that *work*?

MacLeod's satiric vision of Balaclava neatly reflects Americans' conflicting attitudes toward Academe: we believe, we say, heartily, wholly, fully in education; its *really* important--but we also believe that "them that can't, teach"-- and we aren't passionately eager to fund our schools so fully as educators think we should. Herein, perhaps, lies Balaclava's preoccupation with money; even a generous endowment such as that supplied about 190 years ago by the college founder, Balaclava Buggins, can only go so far; after that, it's begging *or*, as MacLeod suggests, the Cookie Works and the Grand Illumination.

Wittingly or not, this author has also put her finger on another major conflict which rages on many, many campuses--are students being schooled to understand their heritage or are they being trained to be good workers? Balaclava's current president, the gigantic, energetic Thorkjeld Svenson, inventor of the Illumination, encourager of profitable research, attempted to resolve that question during the Commencement exercises of 1973, when he "clove a solid oak podium neatly in twain from top to base as he slammed down his fist to emphasize those deathless words, 'Agri isn't a business, it's a culture!'" (*Luck*, 75). Under the leadership of President Svenson, Balaclava strives to teach first of all a way of life; running a close second to that goal is the concept of teaching a *profitable* way of life.

Svenson does it by example--witness the Illumination--and through practical aid. At Balaclava,

> loans and scholarships were not handed out on a platter. Jobs, on the other hand, were plentiful. Any student who needed to earn his way was given the opportunity; anybody who had the opportunity and didn't make it was dropped.
>
> The rationale was simple: farmers were going to have to work hard all their lives anyway. If they couldn't hack it when they were young and strong, why encourage them to hope they'd be able to manage later? (*Luck*, 109-110)

This apparent criticism of the easy financial aid once commonly believed available to students and of various schools' policies of granting extensive periods of "probabíon" is the closest MacLeod ever comes to open attack upon Academe, and those pointed comments are underscored by her description of one of Balaclava's more unusual traditions, one of its most appealing plans.

Balaclava graduates who can demonstrate need and professional skill can "face the future with confidence, knowing the school would make sure they had a future to face," for the college maintains a fund from which outright gifts are "handed out generously" to enable the preservation of family farms and the establishment of small businesses. True to an informal understanding, almost all the gifts are eventually repaid, often "threefold and more" (*Luck*, 110). Many, many Balaclava students, apparently, have had good cause to bless the Cookie Works, the Grand Illumination, and tough, practical President Svenson, and in this way MacLeod balances her most direct social criticism by suggesting what loyal Balaclavians would identify as sound social action.

Through President Svenson's successful dedication to his work, then, MacLeod not only advances her social commentary but also demonstrates that she recognizes the importance of quality education which can be put into quality practice. Balaclava stands for excellence as much as it stands for risibility, and in this fashion the author does much to prevent her academic satires from descending into carping criticism. The portrait of the president serves this purpose in another way also.

President Svenson, like most folk in the Balaclava novels, is really a caricature rather than a fully developed characterization; this device is standard practice in comedies of manners where the characters' behaviors are inflated to illustrate the topic subculture's way of life. Thorkjeld Svenson is truly larger than life--as, perhaps, all college presidents would secretly like to be. In the first Balaclava novel, the president's massive impact is frequently mentioned long before his delayed appearance. When he does appear, he bursts upon the scene,

> filling the tiny hall from side to side and from floor to ceiling. If the hall had been large, the effect would have been the same. No space ever seemed big enough to contain Thorkjeld Svenson. Wearing a sweater and cap of untreated gray sheep's wool knitted for him by his wife, Sieglinde, probably with an assist from the Norns, he looked like a mountain gone astray from its bedrock. (*Rest*, 49)

Strong of back as well as strong of purpose (he is capable of wrenching a door off its hinges or single-handedly lifting the rear wheel of a huge farm wagon off the ground), the president is also fierce of temper and not above threatening his colleagues. As he says--shouts--to Peter Shandy, protagonist of the novels and co-creator of the valuable Balaclava Buster rutabaga: "Damn you Shandy, you've already tried to sabotage the Grand Illumination. If you involve the college in a public scandal ... I'll personally shove a Balaclava Buster straight down your throat and out your other end" (*Rest*, 50).

Svenson doesn't mince words; however, it is suggested, he often minces his staff, and Shandy knows that the threats are not idle. Svenson's attitude will be reflected in the behavior of his subordinates, and Shandy's

> life would be made miserable in countless little ways. His lawn would die, his spruces get bud-worms, his power [emanating from the college-owned plant] would fail and his pipes would freeze and nobody would know why. Secretaries would forget to notify him of faculty meetings, hostesses would absent-mindedly leave him off their guest lists, his students would transfer. At the faculty dining room his food would be served cold and late and

no colleague would dare to share his table. By the end of the next semester, he would either have quit of his own accord or turned into a curmudgeonly recluse. (*Rest,* 21)

He would, perhaps, be forced to imbibe alone--dangerously alone--a college tradition, the "Balaclava Boomerang ... compounded of home-hardened cider and homemade cherry brandy" (*Luck,* 31).

Tough administrator that he is, Svenson is nevertheless somewhat vulnerable. Though Shandy appears to be the only faculty member capable of facing the president down, he is malleable in the hands of his wife, the beautiful, statuesque Sieglinde. She forces him to stick to his diet, to dress warmly (and on occasion properly), and encourages him to relax by watching old John Wayne movies on television or by singing "I'm an Old Cowhand" in Swedish. All her persuasions are effected very tenderly, however, for the couple are, as is made clear, deeply in love.

Happily married himself, Svenson encourages his faculty toward matrimony. Perhaps he considers settled family types to be less apt to take their teaching and research skills off to other academic pastures. In any case, the president fosters a courtship between Peter Shandy and Helen Marsh, a temporary resident of Balaclava Junction, by pressing Helen into a job at the college; the fact that BAC is also acquiring a first-class librarian is not, one can be sure, lost on Prexy. The courtship allows MacLeod to incorporate a standard convention of murder mysteries, a romantic subplot used to allay the horror of the violence and to deepen the plot. The comedy of manners is also served, as Peter instructs Helen in Balaclava tribal lore, and, of course, the portrait of Svenson is extended a bit. His romantic soft spot reveals that Svenson, like all mountains, has feet of clay and that, like many, he has a molten core in more ways than one.

Though Peter Shandy is the protagonist of these stories, Thorkjeld Svenson is their generating force. He propels the unwilling Shandy into the role of amateur detective; he demands the excellence and the intensity which earmark the college, and it is he who keeps Balaclava in funds and thus alive and vigorous. Actually, Svenson is MacLeod's most difficult authorial challenge, and her success in making him funny, vulnerable, and yet powerful is a tribute to her skill.

MacLeod underscores the Svenson caricature in one especially clever fashion, for in many ways Balaclava Agricultural College is a direct reflection of its current president. Balaclava, after all, has feet of dung; its success and stability are grounded firmly in the Cookie Works, and, like Svenson's, its portrait is caricature, not characterization. The use of caricature in both setting and persona is vital to the success of the comedy of manners, for it is a second factor which prevents sarcasm from invading the realm properly belonging to satire.

First of all, of course, the caricatures contribute to the overt humor; they can do what realistic characters cannot--for example, wrench doors off hinges. Secondly, they create a valuable distance between readers and the story. The caricatures are, in some traits, *like* the readers, but they are not *exactly* like; they are merely puppets, not portraits of "real" people. In this way, MacLeod's fictional people act very ob-

viously on a kind of literary stage. The reader recognizes
them as valid, if exaggerated, representatives of life but
does not wholly identify with them. Cast in the role of observer rather than empathizer, the reader is much more likely
to accept the author's social criticism.
   Caricature, then, serves to create distance between reader
and character and to feed the overt humor of the novels. Sym-
biotically, the humor also feeds the distancing, for when
readers can be moved to laugh at society's foibles, they can
accept the validity of the social criticism less painfully,
often, than is the case with many intensely realistic works.
Humor in the hands of a skillful writer like MacLeod also, of
course, helps to undercut the horror of the violence at the
heart of the plots (here, comic relief becomes a major device)
and to keep the comedy of manners a shade more dominant than
the crime puzzle. The structure is intricate, but it works
very well in the treatment of the Balaclava personnel.
   Distancing works just as neatly for Balaclava Agricultural
College as it does in MacLeod's representations of campus
types. How else but by this clever device would she be free
to indulge in teasing, satiric treatment of even such sacred
subjects as intercollegiate sports? In discussing The Annual
Competition of the Balaclava County Draft Horse Association,
MacLeod never once mentions football, basketball, Homecoming,
or Parents' Day, but these rites are clearly in her mind and
in the minds of her readers.
   Competitiveness and school spirit abound as all Balaclavians prepare for such events as the Junior and Senior Plowman's
Contests, the Horseshoe Pitch, and the Stunt Riding exhibition.
As Peter Shandy explains to Helen, about to witness her first
Competition,

>   it's no run-of-the-mill log-pulling contest, it's more like an
>   equine Olympics. We get teams in from all over New England, and
>   it goes on for days. Wait till you see that Grand Opening pro-
>   cession with our Balaclava Blacks [a super-breed of dray horses
>   developed at the college] right up in front of the whole shebang,
>   pulling the big wagon with the Boosters' Band playing! And all
>   the other wagons coming along behind decked out in bunting, with
>   those gorgeous Clydesdales and Percherons and Belgians and Suf-
>   folks groomed till you could see your face in their hides, with
>   their brasses polished like gold and their drivers slicked up in
>   brand-new flannel shirts.... (*Luck*, 22)

It's enough to make anyone burst into the school song led by
President Svenson, the Billy Martin of draft horse games.
Also, winning is enough to ensure more good publicity, to
boost enrollment, and to encourage contributors.
   Campus festivals, faculty, and administration are not,
however, the only forms of campus life to come under MacLeod's
searching eye, for students do not escape examination. Peter
Shandy (perhaps a bit optimistically) believes that "Balaclava
students worked so hard they did little after-hours roister-
ing, except on Saturday evenings" (*Luck*, 50), a situation not
readily apparent on must American campuses. This admirable
preoccupation with their studies does not, however, prevent
fringe groups from developing on campus, and the Vigilant
Vegetarians, locally dubbed the Viggies, represent student

activism. Like student activists everywhere, the Viggies are all too often at odds with the goals of their school; they object to the use of farm animals as food, of course, and "wanted the research directed into new channels, such as training pigs to be potato diggers, security guards, seeing-eye guides, and such, where their natural talents and sagacity could be utilized on a continuing basis rather than their natural succulence exploited as a one-shot deal" (*Luck*, 78).

In *The Luck Runs Out*, the Viggies' determination to further their cause makes them prime suspects in the pignapping of Belinda of Balaclava and in the consequent murder of Flackley the Farrier. This plot complication illustrates the third way in which MacLeod avoids sarcasm while exploiting satire, for she always welds her two literary forms, the comedy of manners and the mystery novel, very firmly together. Amateur detective Shandy's suspicion of the Viggies is a diversion, a distraction. MacLeod's skill as a structuralist extends the red herring device, for *both* the overt humor[4] and the more subtle, steadily unfolding comedy of manners serve as gigantic red herrings in the stories.

ombining gore and laughter in her Balaclava saga, then, Charlotte MacLeod has successfully amalgamated two subgenres of literature, the murder mystery and the comedy of manners. With considerable skill and ingenuity, she has braided together the two strands, each, itself, dual in nature. As is traditional in the crime story, she has introduced two levels of information: the valid, useful, revealing clues and the misleading, distracting red herrings which complicate the plot and tease the intellect. As is traditional in the comedy of manners, she has depicted a symbolic company of players who, through humor and exaggeration, exhibit the values, mores, and foibles of a fairly sizable, fairly significant, readily recognizable subculture. She has merged murder and manners in effective porportions; her bloody comedies of manners are well made--her points are well-taken.

---

[1] Charlotte MacLeod (b. 1922, Bath, New Brunswick, Canada) attended public school in Weymouth, Maine, and the School of Practical Art (now called the Art Institute of Boston). MacLeod works as copy chief and is a member of the corporation of N.H. Miller & Co., Inc., an advertising firm. She also writes under two pseudonyms: Matilda Hughes and Alisa Craig. In addition to her mystery novels for adults, MacLeod has published juveniles as well as stories and articles. Her bibliography includes *Mystery of the White Knight* (1964), *Next Door to Danger* (1965), *The Fat Lady's Ghost* (1968), *Mouse's Vineyard* (1968), *Ask Me No Questions* (1971), *Brass Pounder* (1971), *Astrology for Sceptics* (1972), *King Devil* (1978), *Family Vault* (1979), *We Dare Not Go A-Hunting* (1980), *The Withdrawing Room* (1980)--all as MacLeod; as Hughes: *The Food of Love* (1965), *Headlines for Caroline* (1967); as Craig: *A Pint of Murder* (1980), *Murder Goes Mumming* (1982).
[2] Doubleday. All further references are indicated in the text.
[3] Doubleday. All further references are indicated in the text. As Charlotte MacLeod, she has also published her third Peter Shandy novel--*Wrack and Rune* (1982)--which uses many of the same characters as *Luck* and *Rest* but is not really a campus novel, dealing instead with trouble in Lumpkin Corners.
[4] R.E. Briney, review of *The Luck Runs Out* in *The Mystery Fancier*, 5:5 (September/October 1981), 38.

Spy Series Characters in Hardback
Part XIII

By Barry Van Tilburg

DOSSIER #61: Colonel Duncan Grant.
CREATED BY: Graham Seton (Lt. Col. Graham Seton Hutchinson).
OCCUPATION: At the start of the series Grant is a Colonel in
   Her Majesty's Army. He gets seconded to Military Intelligence in *The W Plan* during WWI. After his retirement from
   the military he is still called upon by his old intelligence boss to solve special problems which need his expertise. He ventures to Africa to become a sheik. He
   helps build the French resistance during WWII. He solves
   the problem of a British workers' strike during WWII. He
   also helps the German underground destroy the Nazis.
ASSOCIATES: Henry Jervois, his Military Intelligence friend;
   Bob Waller, his lifelong friend and helper; Mary, his
   wife; Duncan, his son.
WEAPONS: Can use guns, knives, or sabres, but prefers to use
   his brains.
OTHER COMMENTS: As a soldier, Grant should really welcome the
   war; it is his only real chance to fight. But with his
   association with war he has come to hate it and devotes
   his entire life toward the stopping of any war by any
   means he can. He gets people to follow his ideas by
   creating revolution and rebellion. He stops a revolution
   in England and starts another in Germany. He becomes a
   sheik in Africa to lead the people to greatness instead of
   starting a war.

The W Plan (Butterworth, 1929).
Colonel Grant's Tomorrow (Farrar, 1931).
Scar 77 (Rich & Cowan, 1936).
The K Code Plan (Rich & Cowan, 1937).
According to Plan (Rich & Cowan, 1939).
The V Plan (Eyre & Spottiswoode, 1941).
The Red Colonel (Hutchinson, 1945).

DOSSIER #62: Lanning (Lanny) Prescot Budd.
CREATED BY: Upton Sinclair.
OCCUPATION: Agent for FDR during WWII.
ASSOCIATES: FDR, his boss; Baker, his contact man in the White
   House; Robbie Budd, his father and an airplane maker;
   Beauty Budd, his mother.
WEAPONS: Lanny uses his brains to keep him out of trouble. He

is a true secret agent; no one but the readers, FDR, and
his contact man know he is spying.
OTHER COMMENTS: Lanny, being an art dealer and having grown up
in Europe, is a natural as a spy. He can get in and out
of anywhere, anytime he wants. Being a jet-setter and a
renowned playboy, he has earned the attention of the people
in the know who can tell him things and get things done.
He holds conversations with the heads of American, British,
and French governments. He also talks with Hitler, Goer-
ing, Himmler, and Hess and is a frequent visitor at Karin-
hall and BErchtesgaden. He knows fascist, communist, and
underground agents. The first four books in the series
are not espionage novels; they are about his life before
he became a presidential agent.

World's End (Viking, 1940; Werner Laurie, 1940).
Between Two Worlds (Viking, 1941; Werner Laurie, 1941).
Dragon's Teeth (Viking, 1942; Werner Laurie, 1942).
Wide Is the Gate (Viking, 1943; Werner Laurie, 1943).
Presidential Agent (Viking, 1944; Werner Laurie, 1944).
Dragon Harvest (Viking, 1945; Werner Laurie, 1945).
A World to Win (Viking, 1946; Werner Laurie, 1946).
Presidential Mission (Viking, 1947; Werner Laurie, 1948).
One Clear Call (Viking, 1948; Werner Laurie, 1949).
Oh Shepherd, Speak! (Viking, 1949; Werner Laurie, 1950).
The Return of Lanny Budd (Viking, 1953).

DOSSIER #63: Major "Brains" Cunningham.
CREATED BY: E.P. Thorne.
OCCUPATION: Agent for British Intelligence Department S.
ASSOCIATES: Sir John Crawley, his boss; Alfred Pring, his
right-hand man.
WEAPONS: Automatic pistols.
OTHER COMMENTS: Cunningham is a monocled, wisecracking agent
who solves political murders around the world with the aid
of his batman, Pring. Another recurring character is a
lady named Koi San who tries to kill Cunningham a number
of times. His identification card is accepted in any
country in the free world. People in the series die in
the strangest ways.

The Smile of Cheng Su (Wright & Brown, 1946).
The Face of Inspector Britt (Wright & Brown, 1947).
Sinister Sanctuary (Wright & Brown, 1949).
Justice Is Mine (Wright & Brown, 1950).
The Sahdow of Dr. Ferrari (Wright & Brown, 1951).
The Moon Dance (Wright & Brown, 1953).
Red Bamboo (Wright & Brown, 1954).
Lady with a Gun (Wright & Brown, 1955).
Date with the Departed (Wright & Brown, 1955).
The Bengal Spider Plan (Wright & Brown, 1961).
House of the Fragrant Lotus (Wright & Brown, 1962).
Chinese Poker (Wright & Brown, 1964).
Zero Minus Nine (Wright & Brown, 1964).
The Caribbean Affair (Wright & Brown, 1966).

IT'S ABOUT CRIME by Marvin Lachman

Many years ago, I suggested that P.D. James make a series character of Cordelia Gray, private detective in *An Unsuitable Job for a Woman* (1972). That is exactly what James has done in *The Skull Beneath the Skin* (Scribners, 1982, $13.95), her latest mystery. Gray brings to this book what was lacking in the last James book, *Innocent Blood* (1980)--a decent human being as the central focus of the story. I, for one, wish that Cordelia had played an even greater part in *Skull*. Though she is the detective, she is relatively limited in her time "on stage," and James disappointed me by having her withhold important information from the police without plausible motivation.

Like Ngaio Marsh in *Photo Finish*, James has gone back to one of the time-honored devices in mystery fiction: the murder committed by one of a small group on an isolated island. In this book it is a private theatrical performance that brings some oddly assorted people, including a detective, to the locale. James writes very well indeed, and she shows how the values associated with the best "straight" novels--i.e., good characterization, well realized setting, careful writing, etc.--can enhance the traditional whodunit. She does not succeed entirely, because her plot is not good enough to carry a mystery this long (328 pages), and at times James does get carried away with her skill and overwrites. Still, *Skull* has so much going for it, including the best of the new breed of female detectives, that it can be heartily recommended.

British writers leave us far behind when it comes to quality spy novels. They actually were at their best in the years before John Le Carré came in with the gold. Harper's Perennial Library has reprinted a trio of excellent Cold War mysteries, two of which--Edward Young's *The Fifth Passenger* (1962) and Robert Harling's *The Enormous Shadow* (1955)--I have previously reviewed here. They have just published Michael Innes' *The Man from the Sea* (1955), and, while it is not quite up to the others, it is still very worthwhile. This is Innes in a non-series novel at his "clearest," eschewing the literary allusions which have dragged some of his books down. His emphasis is on action, and the book is suspenseful and very compelling. However, he has not neglected character.

The Man from the Sea starts with a reader-grabbing device. A young Oxford graduate is having a summertime tryst on the Scottish coast with an older, married woman. It is interrupted by the landing from a Russian submarine of a British scientist who had previously defected to the USSR. The scientist says he has escaped from the Russians. Guilt and other emotions cause the young man to try to help the scientist get to London before either Russian agents or British authorities can capture him. Unlike many others, Innes works at making plausible the actions of that staple of spy fiction, the innocent person involved in international intrigue. By convincing this reader, he earned his attention and respect.

Bantam has recently reprinted Rex Stout's second Nero Wolfe novel, *The League of Frightened Men* (1935), and it demonstrates how much better the author was at plotting during the first five years of the series. Many years after a college hazing incident crippled a man who was to go on to be a successful novelist, the original culprits begin dying off mysteriously. Wolfe is hired by the logical suspect, the novelist. Incidentally, there is an unconsciously funny 1937 film version with Walter Connolly as a hot chocolate-drinking Wolfe and Lionel Stander playing Ohio's Archie Goodwin with a Bronx accent. No thonx.

Thanks to Penguin, we can now reread one of the high spots of the 1940's, a decade in which interest in abnormal psychology reached epic proportions. Helen Eustis' *The Horizontal Man* (1946) has many things going for it, including a good ending and a scary atmosphere. Yet the setting, Hollymount College (based on her alma mater, Smith), is just the opposite, with bright college students and professors saying clever things. Perhaps it is just that contrast that makes *The Horizontal Man* such a memorable mystery.

When I was a kid, I didn't read pulps too often. Paperbacks had just come along and seemed more convenient--and respectable. At age twelve I once brought a pulp to school in June, when, at term's end, we were given free reading time. My dear teacher asked me why I was reading "junk." I also recall a used magazine store in the South Bronx which sold pulps at three for a nickel! If I had bought enough of them then, I could retire now. Lately, having purchased the collection of the late Pat Erhardt, I've acquired about 500 pulps, most of which I'll sell, though I'll try to read them first.

So far I've found very few good stories, but they're fun to read. Of the early *Black Mask* writers, except for Hammett and Gardner, Frederick L. Nebel seems the best. His "The Penalty of the Code" (January 1928) and "Raw Law" (September 1928), part of his Crimes of Richmond City series, are simplistic, racist (people are referred to as "dagos" and "dinges") and advocate police brutality, yet they are written with great narrative drive and are surprisingly moving.

Perusing the ads is one of the great things about pulp-reading. Some of those I like best, and I kid you not, included:
1. Anita's Nose Adjustor: "Reshape your nose to beautiful proportions while you sleep."
2. Artificial legs: "Buchstein's fibre limb is soothing to your stump."
3. "False teeth by mail--as little as $6.95."
4. "No more trusses."
5. "Wanted--Part time men."

They'd be funny if they weren't pathetic.

I'm convinced that the world is made up of people who love
the works of Cornell Woolrich and those who can't stand him.
My own family fits that pattern. I've enjoyed his work since
1944. My wife, on the other hand, loathes his work and finds
it very depressing. She couldn't care less about Ballantine's
exciting project of reprinting much of the Woolrich opera.
    Woolrich is great fun to read *if you can suspend disbelief.*
I can not with many other writers, but I've always been able
to with Woolrich. What makes Woolrich so readable for me?
It is not his plotting, which is rudimentary. He hever had a
series detective, and the detection in his stories is not
especially intelligent. The reason seems to be that Woolrich
has made an implicit pact with certain readers willing to meet
him halfway: "Give me your attention and suspend disbelief,
and I will create characters with whom you can identify and
place them in situations of almost non-stop suspense. I will
never bore you."
    Newgate Callendar recently savaged Woolrich's writing
ability, claiming that cliches predominate. Yet, I find the
very type of language he cited to be what carries the reader
along.
    Take *The Black Angel* (1943), arguably Woolrich's best
novel, in which a young wife attempts to prove her husband innocent of the murder for which he has been sentenced to die.
Like so much of Woolrich--e.g., "Three O'Clock" and *Deadline
at Dawn*--this is a story of a protagonist's race against time.
Woolrich describes the slowness of time in terms we can readily understand: "It seemed to have been going on for so long.
This couldn't be the same night, could it? This must have
been some trick arrangement of a week of nights, a month of
them, lumped solidly together without any days in between."
    If I thought about it, I'm sure I would not believe in
Alberta Murray's quest to save her husband, but who thinks
when one is on a roller coaster, and that is exactly where
Woolrich places the reader, grabbing with lines like:

> I took his arm. We must have made a strange-looking couple,
> leaving that place. A woman and a dead man.

> My heart hurt as though a surgeon were taking stitches in it.

> [Regarding a night club:] A bacchanalia at fixed prices. The
> never-ending, never succeeding attempt to hold pain, despair,
> death at bay a little while. A little while longer.

Black Alibi (1942) and *The Black Path of Fear* (1944) are
not as good as *Angel,* but they still have much to recommend
them. *Alibi* contains some good descriptions of a South American city and its inhabitants. Its major weakness is that the
first three-quarters of the book is fairly predictable, albeit
well-written, and is without the element of surprise we expect
in Woolrich. The ending more than makes up for the overly
long descriptions of the victims-to-be, since it is as suspenseful as one could want. And there is that marvelous
language, Woolrichiana. E.g.: "There was a small click, and
his light went out, just as his hopes had long before....
Minutes went by. He looked up once, at the patch of black
over him. It was still night. How long a night lasts sometimes. But not when you are dying."

Black Path is another of Woolrich's Latin American stories, opening in Havana as the protagonist's girl is stabbed in a crowded bar, in his presence. "Then they picked her up and started her on that last long trip she had to take alone.... She'd never liked the dark; I remember her telling me that many times. She'd never liked to be alone in it either. And now she had to go there, where that was all there was, just those two things.... So she went out that way into the black Havana night, without diamonds, without love, without dreams."

He has the seemingly impossible task of proving himself innocent though all evidence points to his having killed the girl. Opium plays a major part in this book, completing the informal trilogy Woolrich began with his novelets "C-Jag" (a.k.a. "Cocaine") and "Marijuana."

If you've already tried Woolrich and didn't like him, there's probably nothing further I can say. But if you've never read him, now is an excellent time to do so. In addition to the three books I've mentioned, Ballantine has also reprinted three which are just as good: *Phantom Lady* (1942), *Black Curtain* (1941), and *Rendezvous in Black* (1945). All are enhanced by the best cover illustrations to come along in years. Mike Nevins succeeded where I failed as a detective and found out the name of the artist, Larry Schwinger of Weehawken, New Jersey.

You won't know which half of the world you fit into until you've tried Cornell Woolrich.

DEATH OF A MYSTERY WRITER

William P. McGivern, in Southern California at age 60 (November 1982). Originally a writer for the pulps, he achieved considerable fame with such excellent novels as *The Big Heat* (1952), *Rogue Cop* (1954), and *Odds Against Tomorrow* (1957). He was married to anthologist-short story writer Maureen Daly.

Frank Swinnerton, in Surrey, England, at age 98 (November 1982). He wrote about sixty novels, several of which fit into the mystery category. He also wrote short stories, two of which won prizes in EQMM's annual contests: "MS in a Safe" (October 1953) and "Soho Night's Entertainment" (January 1957).

REEL MURDERS
MOVIE REVIEWS
by Walter Albert

In 1931, two films were released that are still being shown in theaters and on television: James Whale's *Frankenstein* and Tod Browning's *Dracula*. Their great popularity initiated the horror cycle of the thirties. A third film was released that year whose subject was, like *Frankenstein*, the creation by a brilliant, eccentric scientist of a creature who threatens his creator's life and sanity, but *Dr. Jekyll and Mr. Hyde* is director Rouben Mamoulian's only horror film, and it has languished in relative obscurity. The film's fluid, imaginative camera work, for which Mamoulian was noted, allies it to the best horror/fantasy films of the period as well as to the innovative musicals that were Mamoulian's chief subjects in his long Hollywood career. It may be of some interest to note, in this respect, Whale's direction of the 1936 *Showboat* and to suggest that in their free use of non-realistic elements the musical and horror films of the thirties are not unrelated.

Mamoulian's adaptation, like the other film versions of Robert L. Stevenson's novella, places great emphasis on the laboratory and transformation scenes and, unlike the source, does not attempt to conceal the nature of Hyde's identity from the audience. (In Stevenson's story, Hyde is the evasive criminal whose secret Mr. Utterworth, the lawyer-investigator, wryly calling himself Mr. Seek, sets out to uncover, making of the adventure at once a morality and a detection tale.) The laboratory is the conventional workshop of the thirties' horror film, a classical locus that is at its most poetic and imaginative in Whale's *Bride of Frankenstein*. It is also a dramatic stage which gives some slight plausibility to the drug-induced emergence of the Hyde personality. Mamoulian's principal interest is probably not in the horrific or suspenseful elements of the story, although his film is lacking in neither of these. His Hyde--a curious Simian-Negroid creation that may strike some viewers as a rather blatant ethnic stereotype--is certainly repulsive enough, but I think the director's real subject is the consequences of the release of all inhibitions, his Hyde brooking no interference with any of his immediate needs and desires. This is most evident in the careful portrayal of the apparent distinction between Jekyll, the staid Victorian lover (even if unconventional scientist), and Hyde, the sensual, brutal lover whose pleasure is in a sadistic inflicting of pain on his mistress. And it is in the tactful but powerful depiction of Hyde's relationship with his mistress (marvelously played by Miriam Hopkins) that the originality of this film in its relation to the horror film lies. The male/female relationships in the Hollywood horror films of the period tended to be chaste, unlike the franker treatment in other genre films: the rampant visual/sexual puns in the Busby Berkeley musicals, the poetic physicality of the Tarzan/Jane relationship in the first two MGM Weismuller-O'Sullivan films and Kong's famous--and later edited--undressing of Fay Wray in *King Kong*. If one of the cherished memories--and clichés--is of the monster chasing and sometimes carrying the heroine to a possible but never realized fate worse than death, the sexual play in these films is relatively tame. Not so in Mamoulian's *Jekyll*. One of the best sequences --still memorable and unsettling--is of Hyde's unexpected return to his mistress's chambers and his subsequent vicious teasing before he strangles her in a grim and deadly parody of the sexual embrace. It has often been said that the *Horror of Dracula* (Hammer Films, 1957) made explicit the eroticism of the vampire myth; what should also be pointed out--and perhaps for its irony--is that in the year that Browning's *Dracula* presented the classic version of the gentleman vampire, Mamoulian's night-creature (like Dracula, freest and most powerful in his mistress's bedroom) tortured and teased and sexually abused his lover in a way that the "mainstream" horror film would only dare to follow a quarter of a century later.

The classic horror film has its narrative source in Victorian taboos and the way in which they are circumvented by the monster created in the laboratory or the grave. The vampire is the dark lover, the sensual bringer of pleasure and death, so unlike the correct, cardboard hero. In Mamoulian's film, the hero and the villain inhabit the same body. His Jekyll (Fredric March) has been criticized for his wooden playing, but what has not to my knowledge been pointed out is the way in which, as Hyde increases in strength, Jekyll comes to resemble him. There is a striking scene when Jekyll returns home, free he thinks of Hyde but dressed in the cape and top-hat affected by his other self and in his extravagant gestures more like the exuberant Hyde than the controlled scientist. But, then, Hyde was never far from Jekyll as the scientist pursued his obsession with the separation of the dual self, an obsession whose consequences are finally as destructive as Hyde's natural genius for evil.

Early in the film, before Jekyll effects his first transformation, the good doctor treats a patient in her room. This patient is Ivy, the prostitute Hyde will pursue and kill, and as Jekyll takes his leave of her after they are surprised by his friend Lanyon in a passionate embrace, Ivy whispers seductively, "Come back," and languorously, voluptuously moves her bare leg enticingly back and forth. Mamoulian superimposes the shot of her leg and the echo of her invitation over the following scene as the supposedly blameless Jekyll and his friend walk away from the apartment. Sex and science are both seductive siren calls, and the breaching of limits is fatal for both scientist and lover. Call Mamoulian's *Dr. Jekyll and Mr. Hyde* a morality play, a scientific romance, a monster film with many of the genre's conventions, a psychological flirtation with the mysteries of the self, this superbly crafted and haunting film is an artful extension of the possibilities of

the horror film and it has a power to disturb that still sets
it apart from most other genre films of its time.

SHORT TAKE

One More River. Universal, 1934. Director: James Whale. Script:
R.C. Sherriff, from a John Galsworthy novel. Colin Clive,
Diana Wynyard, Jane Wyatt, Mrs. Patrick Campbell, James Lawton,
Henry Stephenson, C. Aubrey Smith, Henry Daniell, E.E. Clive,
Snub Pollard.

When Diana Wynyard leaves her caddish, sadistic husband,
sneeringly played by Colin Clive, to establish an independent
existence, private detectives report her every move (in particular, a compromising night in the country in a disabled
car with friend and would-be lover James Lawton) to Clive, who
sues her for divorce on grounds of adultery, naming Lawton as
co-respondent. Apart from the casting of his Dr. Frankenstein
and the usual impeccable direction of a fine and varied cast,
the materials of this absorbing melodrama seem somewhat remote
from Whale's imaginative masterpieces: *The Old, Dark House*;
The Invisible Man; and *Bride of Frankenstein*. However, three
brief sequences are reminiscent of those stylish films: Wynyard pulls her hair up into a striking semblance of the Bride's
electrified coiffure; a low-angle shot catches E.E. Clive
looking superciliously toward the bottom of the frame with
Dr. Praetorius's prissy, pursed lips; and, most moving of all,
Mr. Patrick Campbell, slowly climbing an ornate, moodily
lighted staircase (not unlike the staircase in the great hall
of Baron Frankenstein's castle), spectrally intones Lady
Macbeth's exit line, "What's done cannot be undone. To bed,
to bed, to bed," in a cameo scene that sums up unforgettably
Whale's unique feel for the extravagantly theatrical and sardonic, self-conscious mockery. The courtroom scene is splendidly acted and paced and the unlikely team of E.E. Clive and
Snub Pollard, playing comic sleuths, is a delight. Finally,
Diana Wynyard gives an effortless, understated performance
that seems spontaneous and lends credibility to this contemporary story of a rebellion against a class and its taboos, a
subject always of great interest to Whale.

VERDICTS Book Reviews

Max Collins. *The Baby Blue Rip-Off*. Walker, 1983, $11.95.

Welcome, Mallory, to the ranks of the amateur detective/mystery writer.

Mallory--Mal to his friends--is the new reluctant hero in Max Collins's fictive universe. He has direct roots with Collins's best creations: thirty-ish Vietnam veteran, wholesomely lusty, and recently recovered from a long period of directionless living. Now Mallory has settled down to attending college in Iowa, writing his second mystery novel (the first one having just been published), and, as his concession to mankind --and the lusty hospital dietician he's living with--delivering "Meals on Wheels" to elderly town residents one day a week.

It's this philanthropy which causes his trouble: One of Mallory's charges is robbed and accidentally murdered on the night of his delivery. Naturally, he feels compelled to find the murderer.

Along the way he (re)meets an old love from high school-- once the object of fantasy who becomes his partner in almost idyllic sex. There's just one problem: she's married and her husband has hated Mallory from high school days.

Mallory is a classic amateur detective: bumbling, likable, and with just enough of a hint of larceny to not be adverse to breaking into a suspect's place of business in search of stolen goods. The character is believable, no superman, and doesn't make all the right decisions. His one terrible error--but certainly to be expected in a thriller--is climbing into the back of a van used by the killers as they leave on another robbery.

Mallory has all the elements of being a tough-guy hero who has been toned down by the editors. He has no trouble defending himself with his fists but is always in search of a weapon. Perhaps there was a dictum from the publishers that he not have a gun or not provoke violence. No matter, Mallory is tough minded. That's enough for reading pleasure.

Mallory is something of an amalgam of very early Ellery Queen, young Philip Marlowe, and just a hint of another of Collins's characters, Jon from the Nolan series. It's a relief to see a mystery writer portrayed as a sexual being and not as a mere cardboard figure.

Collins, in his eleventh novel, has created his third series character (at least one more Mallory is on the way),

one that can stand with any action/adventure hero. As always
with Collins, the narrative drive is dynamic. There are no
wasted words in a Collins novel. He's a high exponent of the
thriller. The action is swift, the dialogue terse, and the
pleasure immediate. (Jim Traylor)

H.R.F. Keating, ed. *Whodunit? A Guide to Crime, Suspense and
Spy Fiction.* Van Nostrand Reinhold, 1982, $18.95.

This newest of "must have" reference works is edited by
one of England's foremost mystery writers and provides a refreshing British view point of mystery criticism. The only
drawback in the book is that in trying to provide a little of
everything, something had to be excluded. All the entries are
so good the reader is left wanting more.
 First are ten essays about the various forms of crime/
mystery fiction. Most notable are Robert Barnard on "The English Detective Story" and Jessica Mann on "The Suspense Novel."
Other contributors of these essays are Keating, Hillary Waugh
("The American Police Procedural"), Michael Gilbert ("The
British Police Procedural"), Eleanor Sullivan, Michele Slung,
and John Gardner ("The Espionage Novel").
 Next are ten authors in very personalized comments on "How
I Write My Books." Included here are Stanley Ellin, P.D.
James, Patricia Highsmith, Gregory Mcdonald, Len Deighton,
Eric Ambler, and, again, Keating.
 The bulk of the book is taken up with "Writers and Their
Books: A Consumer's Guide." This and the last section on
fictional detectives are the meat and value of the book. Included are dozens of authors, each with a short (50-75 word)
commentary identifying nationality, type of book written, and
notable characteristics. Also, two or three recent or outstanding books by each author are graded on a ten point scale
of characterization, plot, readability, and tension. The comments are mostly non-judgmental while the gradings are obviously
opinions.
 The final section is a biography of ninety detectives and
helpers. Included are the standards such as Albert Campion,
Father Brown, Inspector Wexford, Ellery Queen, Mr. and Mrs.
North, Captain Da Silva, and Matt Helm. The oddities (or non-
detectives) include Professor Moriarty, Magersfontein Lugg
(Campion's companion), and Bunter (Wimsey's butler). The book
is loaded with photos, illustrations, maps, and manuscript
reproductions. In short, it is a volume every mystery fanatic
should have (and will want to have) to bring his reference
shelf up to date. Don't miss it. (Fred Dueren)

Stuart Kaminsky. *Catch a Falling Clown.* St. Martin's, 1981,
 182 pp., $12.95.

 Stuart Kaminsky and Toby Peters are at it again; private
detective to the stars. This time it's Emmett Kelly who is in
need of Toby's assistance. All the ingredients from former
Peters adventures are present in force: Shelly Minck, the disgusting dentist with whom Toby shares his office; Peters' decrepit back with all its aches and pains; inept detection and
solution by dumb luck; cameo appearances by Tinsel Townies;

and a barely submerged sense of humor bordering on parody of
the whole "hard-boiled" genre.
  Kaminsky--a professor in the media field--has strayed from
the area of the film world to render a glimpse of the circus
not generally available to the ticket-buying public. We meet
a lion tamer who when clawed by one of his beasts must show no
pain, a snake lady and her not so friendly pet Abdul, The Fly-
ing--and falling--Tanuccis, and an interested observer named
Alfred Hitchcock.
  With a group like that for suspects, all that is needed
are Toby's own set of clowns and we are ready for a romp
through the sawdust in search of the person that electrocuted
the elephant.
  As you no doubt can tell, this adventure is just as funny
as any of Kaminsky's past efforts. However, after six outings
it must be getting harder to keep the formula fresh. For
Catch a Falling Clown is a formula work, albeit a successful
and funny one. (Alan S. Mosier)

Emma Lathen. *When in Greece*. Berkley, 1970 (first published
  in hard covers in 1969).

  My delay in getting around to a review of this is a direct
result of having had more than the usual difficulty in getting
the book read. That, in turn, was a result of the shabbiness
of paperback book construction over the past couple of decades
and should imply no disappointment nor easy put-downableness
in the book itself.
  The story of Thatcher's invasion of Greece during the
aftermath of the Colonels' coup of the Sixties has to stand
rather near the top in quality for this series. It boasts all
the usual qualities--a gallery of the Sloan's employees from
Thatcher to Miss Corsa, and a growing uncertainty about whether
the progression should be thought of as "down to" or "up to,"
enthusiastically engaged in being themselves; the cleverest
chapter titles in any set of series novels still using that
antique device (if there *are* no others, then my comment should
read "any novels since WWI"; the practice was so common as to
be almost vulgar between the Wars); and there are a few
atypical pleasures to delight the unlikely patron of the
Lathen team who might be beginning to feel Sloaned out.
  Among the regular (or frequent) cast members, Everett
Gabler's curmudgeon role is fleshed out fully here as he becomes almost as important in this book as Thatcher. Another
Sloan employee, Kenneth Nicolls, serves as central character
throughout nearly half the book--a role customarily reserved
for non-regulars who happen to be doing business with the
Sloan. Consequently, Thatcher's role is shrunken, if still
by no means small, and he does remain central to the solution
of the mystery and conclusion of the book. The chapter titles
are culled from the most familiar bits of Greek culture to the
moderately well-read American. Aesop's Fables, myth, mathematical axioms, the noble ruins, later literature's notice of
all such, drama, history (both military political and scientific), philosophy, and even Graeco-American humor are prominent sources. The movies *Never on Sunday* and even more frequently *Zorba the Greek* are the subject of allusions in the
text.

Atypical pleasures include the prominent role of a couple of American female archaeologists, but the archaeological element does not get out of hand as is so frequently the case in mysteries set in modern Greece. Also, there is a different sort of bringing the villain to justice. Typically in this series, the crimes occur in the U.S. (or some other rather settled nation with an established and accepted sense of justice), and all Thatcher must do to assure the proper comeuppance is to turn the villain over to the authorities. With Greece in turmoil and the villain locally "above reproach" (and no more will be said here to possibly give that part of the clever plot away), a different approach is indicated. Thatcher, largely aided and abetted by those American women, hatches a plot so Byzantine that it would have done credit to some of the stingier *Rockford Files* scripts (that's a high compliment, son!) and justice is done.

Highly recommended. If you mean to sample the series, start with this book; if you thing you might read only one more Lathen book, make it this one. (R. Jeff Banks)

George Bradshaw. *Practise to Deceive.* Rupert Hart-Davis, 1962.

A collection of short stories that I'd not previously run across with the unusual connected theme of art forgery. Reminiscent in many ways of O. Henry or (with the French settings of so many of the stories) of Leonard Merrick. Elegant writing and lots of well-constructed twists. Perhaps the cleverest of them all is "Venus Rising," with even one more twist than in the others.

How come this collection isn't better known? (Bob Adey)

Timothy Harris. *Goodnight and Good-bye.* Pan, 1981.

I was frankly a little disappointed with this second, rather muddled adventure of P.I. Thomas Kyd. Anyone who could act so stupidly over the unreliable Laura Cassidy seems an unlikely man to solve this complex affair. Dialogue and some of the action sequences are still very good and Kyd is still a "top ten" P.I., but, oh, how muddled. (Bob Adey)

Michael Gilbert. *Death of a Favorite Girl.* Hodder and Stoughton, 1980 (published in the U.S. as *The Killing of Katie Steelstock* by Harper & Row, 1980).

When Michael Gilbert is in form, there's no better writer of the modern detective novel. And in this one he's in absolutely top form. Around the death of young TV personality Katie Steelstock he weaves a complex web of relationships and personalities. Excellent characterisation with, as always, the police and lawyers in the story particularly well observed.

The courtroom scene is a delight, and the verbal exchanges are a real treat. The red hering and false trails are laid with particular cunning, yet all is satisfactorily explained at the end.

An absolute stunner. The oft-used term "unputdownable" is well merited. (Bob Adey)

The Documents In the Case (Letters)

From John M. Reilly, 293 Washington Ave., Albany, NY 12206:
   I accept your invitation to comment on Linda Toole's letter in TMF 6:6. The most persistent criticism made of *Twentieth Century Crime and Mystery Writers* has been that it omitted some nice, good, important, intriguing, significant, noteworthy, favorite, and even those one reviewer (T.J. Binyon, writing in TLS, June 5, 1981) called writers "on a lower level." Robin Winks, writing in *The New Republic* (October 11, 1980), said he had taken a look at shelves in his library under A and B (assuring us that he keeps only books that strike him as being critically or historically significant to the development of such fiction) and noted 28 authors not present. Well, what is one to do? Apologize or argue? Certainly not, because there would be no end to that. Perhaps what one might do more fruitfully is make some remarks about my editorial principles in compiling the book.
   I confess that I set out without giving a thought to realities of publishing to plan a book that would provide commentary and complete bibliography on every author who ever worked in the genre. I abandoned that idea after a week or two, because a more compelling principle than naming everybody won out. That principle was scholarly usefulness. I don't enclose the term scholarly in quotations, because I am not mocking or half-serious about scholarship; nor do I believe there is a significant gap between the work done on the genre by people who consider themselves fans and those who call themselves scholars. Both groups need reliable guides; both engage in interpretation, though scholars tend to be more complex in their writing of interpretive essays for the obvious reason that their training (self-acquired or gained at the side of a seminar table) has given them a slightly different grammar of criticism. What I aimed to do in conceiving TCC&MW was produce a book that would apply sound scholarly approaches to a body of literature we all take seriously, even as we come at it from different backgrounds. To me that meant, on the one hand, providing the growing field of popular culture studies ways to get beyond the better-known books and the writers pushed by the publishing houses. I imagined, for example, that articles in the *Journal of Popular Culture* might be more varied and probably better if academics drawn to study of crime literature could find their way off the main boulevard. On the other hand, I hoped, too, that fanzine writers

and devoted readers of the genre would find the reference book
a means to explore more and more of the side streets, while
also having the benefit of sound bibliographical principles.
   With that general aim in mind most everything else followed
readily. I determined that the book would be author-centered.
Apparently that bothers readers and reviewers considerably.
T.J. Binyon (cited above) said there should have been an index
of titles, and space for it could have been gained by limiting
bibliographies to crime titles alone. Joyce Toscan, writing
in a professional librarian's journal, said a listing of characters might well have been included since for many people
characters such as Peter Wimsey are better known than their
creator (!). To be sure, Al Hubin has met these needs, and
knowledge of his marvelous accomplishment had some bearing on
my thinking, and that of the publisher. Above all, though, my
intention, as I say, was to produce an author-centered book.
It is the professional writer whose skills of narrative craft
and ability to solve the interesting technical problems presented by the need to innovate against a background of highly
familiar conventions who is the source of our pleasure. It
can be fun to play that Holmes is alive, or was until recently,
just as it is interesting to ask if people really did live
happily ever after. Let us not forget, however, that we are
talking about fiction, texts that provoke such fantasy games
because of an author's skill. So, then, I resolved that the
writers were to be represented in the book primarily.
   It followed, therefore, that bibliographies ought to
represent the writers' *total* output. If they have written
travel books, straight novels, screenplays for which they received credit, etc., users of the book should know about the
other publications in order to see the full range of accomplishment. Possibly this would show as well what place crime
writing has in the writer's total output (e.g., is he/she incidentally a crime writer but mainly a western writer, or,
does this person maybe write expertly in science?). Study and
interpretation can be helped by this sort of information I am
sure. Similarly, the decision to list uncollected short stories was an attempt to show total output and to acknowledge
that many writers made important contributions in shorter
forms of narrative, even though fashion today implies the
novel-length narrative is the highest form of fiction.
   Selections of writers for inclusion in TCC&MW was under-
taken with the help of advisers, all of whom are listed in the
book. With their help I prepared several lists of hundreds
and hundreds of writers, asking each time I circulated the
lists for arguments for and against inclusion. My directions
were to tell who ought to be in the book because of quality,
historical importance, or important contribution to the genre.
I won't blame the advisers for final choices, though without
their expert aid I couldn't have reached the point of making
final choices. I thank them for their help and have acknowl-
edged some extraordinary contributions in the book. I will
take personal responsibility for these guides in making
choices. First, I decided that the emphasis would be on
writers who really worked hard in the genre, not on "famous
writers" who might have done a single book. As one professional writer wrote to me, you don't want to give a begrudging
pat on the back to the genre by pointing out that even "greats"
now and then indulge. He was right. I wanted to focus atten-

tion on writers who seriously worked the form. After that, it became a matter of space. We cut the size of essays we requested in order to increase the number of authors included. We cover only 614, and since the book has come out numbers of authors have produced so much significant work that it is clear that they should have been seen as comers.

Let me add now another word about the book, a word also provoked by Mr. Binyon's review. In a way characteristic of English academics, he criticizes the American scholarship industry. We list the holdings of manuscripts in libraries. Need they be preserved, he asks, when we have their printed works? Will future graduate students be mining these stores for doctoral dissertations, he sneers. Why not, I reply. The manuscripts of professional authors are important as a means of showing us something about the process of composition. That is as true for writers of crime and mystery fiction as it is for Alexander Pope. Doctoral studies of so-called popular writers can be as useful to our understanding of literature (for example, uses of language signs) as is the writing of other authors. It is, I believe, a mistake of a serious sort to belittle the crime genre by describing it as mere entertainment. As I try to say in the preface to TCC&MW, these narratives manifest a fundamental human enterprise--story telling. Surely it is entertaining, but it is also worthy of attention for the shaping of attitudes or values, the presentation of "myths," the evidence of language, the commentary it obliquely offers. The best way into such interesting problems is through the creators of the narratives, the authors. That is my view, and, because it may not have been as evident as I hoped it would be, I belabor you with this long letter.

May I close the circle in conclusion and return to Linda Toole's letter? She asks, as so many have, where are the important writers such as .... I offer a consolation. The book is going to be revised every five years. New authors will be added, some old ones dropped. Essays will be updated, some improved, I hope. The publication date for the second edition is 1985. That means work will begin in late 1983, or early 1984. I promise there will be some new favorites in the second edition, and the third. I welcome all suggestions, and it is not too soon to start volunteering to contribute. I cannot promise selection for quite a while, nor will I promise anybody can get rich writing for the new editions of the book. I will promise that if you believe the genre deserves the best scholarly attention (remember I don't use the word in any exclusive way), you can have a hand in the book.

From Steve Stilwell, 3004 E. 25th St., Minneapolis, MN 55406:
This is a letter that I didn't particularly want to write, which is one of the reasons it has taken me so long to do it. (The other reason being my basic procrastination.) However, in the interest of future indexers, I feel that I must make some comments about Charles K. Cook's five-year index to TMF.

Let me preface this by saying that, as the main compiler of the ten-year index to TAD, I fully realize and appreciate all of the work that Mr. Cook put into his index and the pride that I'm sure he takes in it. I do feel that there are some serious problems with it that make it difficult to use.

Where to start? First, with the fact that the books re-

viewed are listed only under the *reviewer's* name, so if you
want to know if a book was reviewed and you don't know who may
have reviewed it, you're out of luck. Not so, says GMT. You
have the yearly index to books reviewed, started by Jeff
Meyerson and continued by Dave Doerrer. But I submit that a
comprehensive five-year index to a magazine should not make it
necessary to consult back issues of the magazine (which may or
may not be easily available) to find out if a book has been
reviewed. An index should be judged not only on its accuracy,
but also on its ease of use.
    Which brings me to a point of contention with the editor
of this magazine. If an index, whether it be for a year or
for five years, is not going to be in the final issue of the
year or volume indexed, it is my belief that it should be
published as a separate entity. Again, for ease of use, as
this allows the index to be more accessible and does not neces-
sitate remembering in what issue of the current volume lies
the index to the preceding volume. This is not always easy to
make happen or good business sense, but from a research stand-
point it is the only way.
    Anyway, back to Mr. Cook's index. My second cavil (and
probably last, as this letter has gone on much too long) is
about the subject indexing of the letters. When Guy first
told me that Mr. Cook was subject indexing the letters I was
very pleased, as this was and continues to be the most difficult part of the TAD indexes. How to decide when something
merits a subject heading, what subject heading to use, when is
a subject discussed in great enough detail to merit including,
all of these questions were and are very difficult to answer.
Mr. Cook's answer was not to create subject headings at all,
but simply to list the subjects discussed in a person's letter
under that person's name and letter citation. Now, this makes
fascinating reading, but as far as being helpful in finding a
particular subject, the mind boggles. I submit that the subject listing, "Comments on almost everything in TMF," is
nothing if not useless as a research guide.
    But enough! I hope that Mr. Cook understands what I'm
trying to say and I hope that I've said it in such a way that
he will not be discouraged, but will continue to do this type
of work for the mystery field. God knows we need people who
are willing to take on this type of scut work. (Just ask John
Nieminski.) There needed to be a five-year index to TMF, and
better Mr. Cook's effort than none at all. Thanks, Mr. Cook.

From David Doerrer, 4626 Baywood Circle, Pensacola, FL 32504:
    I see from my files that it's about time for what seems to
have become my annual letter to Ye Editor. As one can easily
see from Charles Cook's index, my letter writing has dropped
off dramatically these past two years. Despite the lack of
evidence via comment, I'm still reading and enjoying TMF.[...]
    The first five issues of Volume 6 have been a real treat,
with something for everyone. Marvin Lachman's columns, Steve
Lewis's reviews, and the reviews by others are such well established, quality features that I suspect they would elicit comment only in their absence. I do particularly appreciate
Marv's necrologies, sad as it is to note the passing of some
of my favorite authors.
    All of the other articles were, to me at least, remarkable

for the quality of both their scholarship and their readability. I do not believe that serious and informative writing has to be dull, but unfortunately a lot of it is. I will read a dull article if I need the information it contains, but not otherwise. TMF's articles have been consistently both informative and enjoyable.
 I was very pleased to read that Barry Van Tilberg is going to follow his series on spy characters in hardback with one on those in paperback and then very disappointed not to see the first installment in 6:4 as promised. I hope he hasn't changed his mind? [*He hasn't.*]
 Charles K. Cook deserves the thanks of all of us for his five-year cumulative index. Having done just the annual index to *The Poisoned Pen* for the second year, I know how much effort is involved. As the compiler of a major index said to me recently, "What can you say about an index, unless there's something wrong with it?" One thing is that journal indexes are invaluable to the researcher; few things offer more frustration than a serial run whose contents are inaccessible save by paging through each issue. With that said, I do have two minor quibbles. The first is that Mr. Cook's index would have been even more useful had the books reviewed been included under title, or author and title, in addition to their appearance under the name of the reviewer. I do realize that this would both have duplicated the annual index and have considerably increased the length of the Cook index, but I think it would have been worth it. The second quibble is even less important. For convenience sake, I would have liked to see the Cook index either as a separate or in 6:6, but this is really nit-picking!
 I'll wind this up by saying that I'm truly amazed that you have been able to continue to put out issues of such consistent quality--the printing of 6:3 was not "poor," and I wear bifocals--in the face of the problems you've experienced this past year, not to mention the dollar cost which I shudder even to contemplate. You could hardly be blamed if, as other fanzine publishers have done, you had simply thrown up your hands in disgust and quit. I am very thankful that you did not.
 [*I'll respond to Steve's and David's comments together. First off, I take full responsibility for any shortcomings there may be in Charlie's index. He constantly asked me for suggestions from beginning to end and would have complied cheerfully with any suggestions that I made. Therefore, if there are shortcomings in the index, they are there because I failed to suggest that they be eliminated. Second, I think that Steve rather overstates the difficulty of using the index to find subjects discussed in letters. True, the index as a whole does need to be scanned, but the letters are quite easy to pick out. It's not as easy to use as it could be, but it's not all that difficult, either. Third, I don't have the correspondence before me, but I believe that Charlie did indeed ask if I wanted him to cross index the books reviewed by title and author as well as by reviewer, and I rejected the idea because it would have all but doubled the size of the index. My fault again. Also my fault is the fact that the index was published as a number in the volume rather than as a separate booklet. I doubted that there would be enough people willing to shell out extra money for an index to cover the cost of printing it by itself, so I decided to run it in 6:5. I'm not*

convinced that it was a mistake.]

From Jiro Kimura, 2-10-11 Shimo-ochiai, #A202, Shinjuku-ku,
Tokyo:
   Would you tell me who won the Fourth Nero Wolfe Award and
what's happening to the Wolfe Pack *Gazette*. I thought you,
Brownstone Books, had taken over the *Gazette*.[...]
   [*As a matter of fact, I have tried on several occasions to
get someone--anyone--who is connected with the* Gazette *to talk
with me about taking it over, but I've never gotten any re-
sponse. I'd still be interested in doing it, but I'm tired
of writing letters that go unanswered.*]
   P.S. The real name of James Melville, who wrote *A Sort of
Samurai* (St. Martin's, 1981, reviewed in TMF 6:6, p. 34), is
Peter Martin. He works at the British Consulate in Tokyo.
I've nothing to do with "Jiro Kimura," a flashy, westernized
playboy in the series. I wish I were him.

From Ola Str∅m, postboks 2124, N-7001, Trondheim, Norway:
   You seem to have got a discussion on how to evaluate puzzle novels after publishing Bleiler's comments on *The Peacock
Feather Murders*. Now Bleiler is not the first trying to pin-
point the impossibilities in books by John Dickson Carr. In
the Spring 1981 issue of TAD, James Kingman has things to say
about *The Crooked Hinge*.
   I'm not sure about Mr. Bleiler needing a spokesman, but in
TMF 6:6 he does put out a call for comments. I support the
opinion that we should not make a habit of revealing the solu-
tions to mystery stories, especially in books or articles intended as introductory reading. In a Norwegian book on crime
and crime fiction published this fall, the authors manage to
kill, among other books, Carr's *Nine—And Death Makes Ten* in
their capsule presentation by using this effective method. On
the other hand, when analysing literature it is only natural
to stress the same elements that the various authors stress.
In a puzzle the important factor is the plot. A plot has two
sides, the premise and the solution. And there you are.
   As a reader who enjoys impossible crimes and other intricate plots, I still think that we should be more willing to
examine in depth the quality of the plots presented to us by
the authors. It would be ridiculous to use character description as a basis for evaluating the works of John Dickson Carr,
but to discuss the coherence of his plots must be quite per-
tinent. More often than we should like to think, famous plots
may fall through if scrutinized *on their authors' own premises*.
This should not happen unnoticed. If we believe that good
plotting is essential in certain types of mystery fiction,
then--in our own interest--we must be willing to examine what
constitutes good plotting. And that includes comparing solution with premise, I am afraid.
   Therefore I look forward to more articles by Bleiler in
the same vein. (Now, that is not the pure truth. What I
really want him to produce is his *Guide to Supernatural Fiction*, which has been postponed. And we still await *Before Poe*
from Firebell Books, do we not?)

From Bob Adey, 7 Highcroft Avenue, Wordsley, Stourbridge, West Midlands, DY8 5LX, England:
[...] May I continue by harking back to the great cricket controversy? Having played the game since boyhood, I think I can explain the misunderstanding over bowling/throwing. The equivalent of the baseball pitcher in cricket is the bowler, who bowls with an overarm action where the arm does not bend at wrist or elbow. Underarm bowling is not illegal, but it is only used by small children before they learn the faster, overarm style. In addition, the cricket outfielders ("on the boundary," "in the deep," etc.) have the same objective as their counterparts in baseball--to return the ball as quickly as possible. Hence they use exactly the same throwing style as in baseball.
  The feat described by Carr in his book would certainly be difficult, but it would not be impossible for a cricketer who had developed his particular skill to that high degree.
  I enjoyed the Rex Stout hoax enormously--by far the most skilful yet perpetrated in the various fanzines. However, I couldn't get past the D.E. Funct pseudonym. For me that was the give away. (However, I was not entirely confident--so much so that I actually wrote to one of my Australian contacts and asked him to look out for the book!)
  Excellent new cover, though I had become rather fond of the old one.

From Marv Lachman, 34 Yorkshire Drive, Suffern, NY 10901:
  Vol. 5, No. 6 was really outstanding, especially Walter Albert's column, the reviews, and the letters. Is the movie Jim Goodrich is looking for *Rogue Cop* from the William McGivern novel? I also agree with Jim regarding Dennis O'Keefe, especially his role in *T-Men*. Jim in turn agrees with me regarding my criticism of Ev Bleiler's *Peacock* article.
  I was glad to see some controversy raised in your letter column, but I'm sure Mr. Bleiler and I disagree from positions of mutual respect. Though I questioned the limited audience for his review, I did not mean to imply that it was not worthwhile doing. A TMF reader who has a copy of the Dickson book would do well to read it now so he can compare his opinion with Beiler's. Though I like Carr, I don't think he (or anyone) should be above criticism. Again, I was only questioning how many TMF readers would spend time on a six-page analysis of a book they either had not read or had read long ago. Mr. Bleiler's detailed plot analysis would help, but it would not be enough. I, for one, was incredibly lucky in having finished the book a few days before TMF arrived.
  Re the matter of Carr's deception about the number of shots fired behind the door: Mr. Bleiler did not complete the sentence he quoted, namely: "A heavy revolver had been fired twice behind that door; and, while the echoes of the shots were settling, Pollard heard his wrist-watch loudly." The part I underline, which he did not quote, indicated to me that it was only in the mind of Pollard, who was fooled, that the shots were heard.
  Regarding the cricket bowling question, I hope Jon Breen will comment since he is one of the few Americans I know who has a knowledge of cricket. [*Let's not be provincial, Marv; TMF's readership is international. See Bob's letter above.*]

To sum up and paraphrase Voltaire: I may not agree with
everything you write, Ev, but I'll read all of it because
you're one of the most astute editors and critics around.

From Al Mosier, 75 Oak Street, Stonham, MA 02180:
I love the new cover that appeared on 6:6. The artwork is
first rate!
Must admit, I was completely taken in by the Tod Hunter
bit. Am only a closet Wolfe enthusiast, so maybe I have an
excuse. However, *D.E. Funct* should have put me wise.
[...] Sorry to see that Steve Lewis is suffering from
Burnout. Hope that you can twist his arm for a couple of reviews each issue. My goal for 1983 is to see if I can send
you at least two reviews for each issue. (I would love to
help fill up the gap!)

From Jim Tinsman, 431 Caloric Circle, Topton, PA 19562:
I have about twelve copies (originals) of TMN #9 (The Rex
Stout Memorial Issue). $6.00 will get anyone a copy for as
long as the supply lasts; if you want first class mail delivery, add $2.00. I also have copies of TMN #10 (Rendell
issue) for $5.00 ppd ($1.50 extra for first class), TMN #11
(EQ index) for $4.75 ppd ($1.25 extra for first class), and
TMN #12 (Crossen issue) for $5.00 ($1.50 extra for first
class). All are originals. I have earlier issues but cannot
get at them at the moment. If anyone is interested AND patient, let me know of the interest and, ultimately, I'll
respond. While I have a bookstore (in Kutztown, PA), my
living is earned as a college teacher in anthropology, and
those demands on my time take precedence.

From Alette L. Hill, 275 29th St., Boulder, CO 80303:
I am teaching a course in detective fiction by women this
spring at Metropolitan State College in Denver.[...] I was
much intrigued by the remarks of two of your readers (both
women, I think) who can't stand to read mysteries written by
women. They don't explain why. Perhaps you could elicit an
article by one of them (e.g., Melinda Reynolds, p. 42 of 6:6)
as to what turns them off about women writers. It seems to
me that they vary widely in style and approach. This subject
intrigues me. [*How about it, Melinda?*]

From Mike Nevins, 7045 Cornell, University City, MO 63130:
I'm sure several readers have already told you this, but
the movie in which Lee Marvin threw the hot coffee in Gloria
Graham's face was *The Big Heat* (1953), based on the novel by
the late William P. McGivern.

From Charles Shibuk, 2084 Bronx Park East, Bronx, NY 10462:
As a postscript to Walter Albert's discussion of Clouzot's
grim *Le Corbeau*, I might add that this film was effectively
remade by Twentieth Century—Fox as *The Thirteenth Letter*,
with Charles Boyer and Linda Darnell, and released in 1951.

www.ingramcontent.com/pod-product-compliance
Lightning Source LLC
Chambersburg PA
CBHW031308060426
42444CB00032B/815